D1670944

How to Divorce
A Narcissist or a Psychopath

1st EDITION

Sam Vaknin

The Author is NOT a Mental Health Professional.
The Author is certified in Counselling Techniques.

Editing and Design:
Lidija Rangelovska

A Narcissus Publications Imprint
Prague & Haifa 2018

To get FREE updates of this book JOIN the Narcissism Study List. To JOIN, visit our Web sites:
http://www.narcissistic-abuse.com/narclist.html or
http://groups.yahoo.com/group/narcissisticabuse

Visit the Author's Web site   http://www.narcissistic-abuse.com

Facebook   http://www.facebook.com/samvaknin

YouTube channel   http://www.youtube.com/samvaknin

Buy other books and video lectures about pathological narcissism and relationships with abusive narcissists and psychopaths here:

http://www.narcissistic-abuse.com/thebook.html

Buy Kindle books here:

http://www.amazon.com/s/ref=ntt_athr_dp_sr_1?_encoding=UTF8&field-author=Sam%20Vaknin&search-alias=digital-text&sort=relevancerank

CONTENTS

*Throughout this book click on blue-lettered text to navigate
to different chapters or to access online resources*

Online index

Go here: http://www.narcissistic-abuse.com/siteindex.html

CHAPTER ONE

Divorcing the Narcissist and the Psychopath

Points to Ponder

How to cope with your narcissist throughout the prolonged process? How to expose the manipulations of the narcissist in court?
What to expect of the narcissist as your divorce unfolds? Will he become violent and vindictive?

Question: I finally mustered the courage and determination to divorce him. But he refuses to let go, he threatens me and stalks and harasses me. I am sometimes afraid for my life. He is also a convincing pathological liar. I am afraid he will turn the judge against me...

Answer: I am not a divorce lawyer and, therefore, cannot relate to the legal aspects of your predicament. But I can elaborate on three important elements:

1. How to cope with your narcissist throughout the prolonged process?
2. How to expose the manipulations of the narcissist in court?
3. What to expect of the narcissist as your divorce unfolds? Will he become violent?

Divorce is a life crisis – and more so for the narcissist. The narcissist stands to lose not only his spouse but an important Source of Narcissistic Supply. This results in narcissistic injury, rage, and all-pervasive feelings of injustice, helplessness and paranoia.

How to Cope with the Narcissist, Psychopath, Bully, or Stalker

If he has a rage attack – rage back. This will provoke in him fears of being abandoned and the resulting calm will be so total that it might seem eerie. Narcissists are known for these sudden tectonic shifts in mood and in behaviour.

Mirror the narcissist's actions and repeat his words. If he threatens - threaten back and credibly try to use the same language and content. If he leaves the house - leave it as well, disappear on him. If he is suspicious - act suspicious. Be critical, denigrating, humiliating, go down to his level. Faced with his mirror image - the narcissist always recoils.

The other way is to abandon him and go about reconstructing your own life. Very few people deserve the kind of investment that is an absolute prerequisite to living with a narcissist. To cope with a narcissist is a full time, energy and emotion-draining job, which reduces the persons around the narcissist to insecure nervous wrecks.

Return

CHAPTER TWO

What is Abuse?

Violence in the family often follows other forms of more subtle and long-term abuse: verbal, emotional, psychological sexual, or financial.

It is closely correlated with alcoholism, drug consumption, intimate-partner homicide, teen pregnancy, infant and child mortality, spontaneous abortion, reckless behaviours, suicide, and the onset of mental health disorders.

Most abusers and batterers are males – but a significant minority are women. This being a "Women's Issue", the problem was swept under the carpet for generations and only recently has it come to public awareness. Yet, even today, society – for instance, through the court and the mental health systems – largely ignores domestic violence and abuse in the family. This induces feelings of shame and guilt in the victims and "legitimizes" the role of the abuser.

Violence in the family is mostly spousal – one spouse beating, raping, or otherwise physically harming and torturing the other. But children are also and often victims – either directly, or indirectly. Other vulnerable familial groups include the elderly and the disabled.

Abuse and violence cross geographical and cultural boundaries, and social and economic strata. It is common among the rich and the poor, the well-educated and the less so, the young and the middle-aged, city dwellers and rural folk. It is a universal phenomenon.

Abusers exploit, lie, insult, demean, ignore (the "silent treatment"), manipulate, and control.

There are many ways to abuse. To love too much is to abuse. It is tantamount to treating someone as an extension, an object, or an instrument of gratification. To be over-protective, not to respect privacy, to be brutally honest, with a sadistic sense of humour, or consistently tactless – is to abuse.

To expect too much, to denigrate, to ignore – are all modes of abuse. There is physical abuse, verbal abuse, psychological abuse, sexual abuse. The list is long. Most abusers abuse surreptitiously. They are "stealth abusers". You have to actually live with one in order to witness the abuse.

There are four important categories of abuse:

[Click here for A Classification of Abusive Behaviours]

Overt Abuse

The open and explicit abuse of another person. Threatening, coercing, beating, lying, berating, demeaning, chastising, insulting, humiliating, exploiting, ignoring ("silent treatment"), devaluing, unceremoniously discarding, verbal abuse, physical abuse and sexual abuse are all forms of overt abuse.

Covert or Controlling Abuse

Abuse is almost entirely about control. It is often a primitive and immature reaction to life circumstances in which the abuser (usually in his childhood) was rendered helpless. It is about re-exerting one's identity, re-establishing predictability, mastering the environment – human and physical.

The bulk of abusive behaviours can be traced to this panicky reaction to the remote potential for loss of control. Many abusers are hypochondriacs (and difficult patients) because they are afraid to lose control over their body, its looks and its proper functioning. They are obsessive-compulsive in an effort to subdue their physical habitat and render it foreseeable. They stalk people and harass them as a means of "being in touch" – another form of control.

To the abuser, nothing exists outside himself. Meaningful others are extensions, internal, assimilated, objects – not external ones. Thus, losing control over a significant other – is equivalent to losing control of a limb, or of one's brain. It is terrifying.

Independent or disobedient people evoke in the abuser the realization that something is wrong with his worldview, that he is not the centre of the world or its cause and that he cannot control what, to him, are internal representations.

To the abuser, losing control means going insane. Because other people are mere elements in the abuser's mind – being unable to manipulate them literally means losing it (his mind). Imagine if you suddenly were to find out that you cannot manipulate your memories or control your thoughts... Nightmarish!

In his frantic efforts to maintain control or re-assert it, the abuser resorts to a myriad of fiendishly inventive stratagems and mechanisms. Here is a partial list:

Unpredictability and Uncertainty (Intermittent Reinforcement)

The abuser acts unpredictably, capriciously, inconsistently and irrationally. This serves to render others dependent upon the next twist and turn of the abuser, his next inexplicable whim, upon his next outburst, denial, or smile.

The abuser makes sure that *he* is the only reliable element in the lives of his nearest and dearest – by shattering the rest of their world through his seemingly insane behaviour. He perpetuates his stable presence in their lives – by destabilizing their own.

Tip

Refuse to accept such behaviour. Demand reasonably predictable and rational actions and reactions. Insist on respect for your boundaries, predilections, preferences, and priorities.

Disproportional Reactions

One of the favourite tools of manipulation in the abuser's arsenal is the disproportionality of his reactions. He reacts with supreme rage to the slightest slight. Or, he would punish severely for what he perceives to be an offence against him, no matter how minor. Or, he would throw a temper tantrum over any discord or disagreement, however gently and considerately expressed. Or, he would act inordinately attentive, charming and tempting (even over-sexed, if need be).

This ever-shifting code of conduct and the unusually harsh and arbitrarily applied penalties are premeditated. The victims are kept in the dark. Neediness and dependence on the source of "justice" meted and judgement passed – on the abuser – are thus guaranteed.

Tip

Demand a just and proportional treatment. Reject or ignore unjust and capricious behaviour.

If you are up to the inevitable confrontation, react in kind. Let him taste some of his own medicine.

Dehumanization and Objectification (Abuse)

People have a need to believe in the empathic skills and basic good-heartedness of others. By dehumanizing and objectifying people – the abuser attacks the very foundations of human interaction. This is the "alien" aspect of abusers – they may be excellent imitations of fully formed adults but they are emotionally absent and immature.

Abuse is so horrid, so repulsive, so phantasmagoric – that people recoil in terror. It is then, with their defences absolutely down, that they are the most susceptible and vulnerable to the abuser's control. Physical, psychological, verbal and sexual abuse are all forms of dehumanization and objectification.

Tip

Never show your abuser that you are afraid of him. Do not negotiate with bullies. They are insatiable. Do not succumb to blackmail.

If things get rough – disengage, involve law enforcement officers, friends and colleagues, or threaten him (legally).

Do not keep your abuse a secret. Secrecy is the abuser's weapon.

Never give him a second chance. React with your full arsenal to the first transgression.

Abuse of Information

From the first moments of an encounter with another person, the abuser is on the prowl. He collects information. The more he knows about his potential victim – the better able he is to coerce, manipulate, charm, extort or convert it "to the cause". The abuser does not hesitate to misuse the information he gleaned, regardless of its intimate nature or the circumstances in which he obtained it. This is a powerful tool in his armoury.

Tip

Be guarded. Don't be too forthcoming in a first or casual meeting. Gather intelligence.

Be yourself. Don't misrepresent your wishes, boundaries, preferences, priorities, and red lines.

Do not behave inconsistently. Do not go back on your word. Be firm and resolute.

Impossible Situations

The abuser engineers impossible, dangerous, unpredictable, unprecedented, or highly specific situations in which he is sorely needed. The abuser makes sure that his knowledge, his skills, his connections, or his traits are the only ones applicable and the most useful in the situations that he, himself, wrought. The abuser generates his own indispensability.

Tip

Stay away from such quagmires. Scrutinize every offer and suggestion, no matter how innocuous.

Prepare backup plans. Keep others informed of your whereabouts and appraised of your situation.

Be vigilant and doubting. Do not be gullible and suggestible. Better safe than sorry.

Financial Abuse

Abusers are control freaks, paranoid, jealous, possessive, and envious. They are the sad products of early childhood abandonment by parents, caregivers, role models, and/or peers. Hence their extreme abandonment anxiety and insecure attachment style. Fostering financial dependence in their nearest and dearest is just another way of making sure of their continued presence as Sources of Narcissistic Supply (attention.) He who holds the purse strings holds the heart's strings. Reducing other people to begging and cajoling also buttresses the narcissist's grandiose fantasy of omnipotence and provides him with a somewhat sadistic gratification.

Tip

You should never allow yourself to be irrevocably separated from your family of origin and close friends. You should maintain your support network and refuse to become a part of the abuser's cult-like shared psychosis.

You should make sure that you have independent sources of wealth (a trust fund, real estate, bank accounts, deposits, securities) and sustainable sources of income (a job, rental income, interest and dividends, royalties).

Above all: you should not share with your abusive intimate partner the full, unmitigated details of your life and critical bits of information such as banking passwords and safe box access codes.

Control and Abuse by Proxy

If all else fails, the abuser recruits friends, colleagues, mates, family members, the authorities, institutions, neighbours, the media, teachers – in short, third parties – to do his bidding. He uses them to cajole, coerce, threaten, stalk, offer, retreat, tempt, convince, harass, communicate and otherwise manipulate his target. He controls these unaware instruments exactly as he plans to control his ultimate prey. He employs the same mechanisms and devices. And he dumps his props unceremoniously when the job is done.

Another form of control by proxy is to engineer situations in which abuse is inflicted upon another person. Such carefully crafted scenarios of embarrassment and humiliation provoke social sanctions (condemnation, opprobrium, or even physical punishment) against the victim. Society, or a social group, becomes the instrument of the abuser.

Tip

Often the abuser's proxies are unaware of their role. Expose him. Inform them. Demonstrate to them how they are being abused, misused, and plain used by the abuser.

Trap your abuser. Treat him as he treats you. Involve others. Bring it into the open. Nothing like sunshine to disinfest abuse.

Ambient Abuse and Gaslighting

The fostering, propagation and enhancement of an atmosphere of fear, intimidation, instability, unpredictability and irritation. There are no acts of traceable explicit abuse, nor any manipulative settings of control. Yet, the irksome feeling remains, a disagreeable foreboding, a premonition, a bad omen. This is sometimes called "gaslighting".

In the long-term, such an environment erodes the victim's sense of self-worth and self-esteem. Self-confidence is shaken badly. Often, the victim adopts a paranoid or schizoid stance and thus renders himself or herself exposed even more to criticism and judgement. The roles are thus reversed: the victim is considered mentally deranged and the abuser - the suffering soul.

Tip

Run! Get away! Ambient abuse often develops to overt and violent abuse. You don't owe anyone an explanation - but you owe yourself a life. Bail out.

Appendix: A Classification of Abusive Behaviours

Abusive conduct is not a uniform, homogeneous phenomenon. It stems and emanates from multiples sources and manifests in a myriad ways. Following are a few useful distinctions which pertain to abuse and could serve as organizing, taxonomical principles (dimensional typologies) in a kind of matrix.

Overt vs. Covert Abuse

Overt abuse is the open and explicit, easily discernible, clear-cut abuse of another person in any way, shape, or form (verbal, physical, sexual, financial, psychological-emotional, etc.).

Covert abuse revolves around the abuser's need to assert and maintain control over his victim. It can wear many forms, not all of which are self-evident, unequivocal, and unambiguous.

Explicit vs. Stealth or Ambient Abuse (Gaslighting)

A more useful distinction, therefore, is between explicit (manifest, obvious, indisputable, easily observable even by a casual spectator or interlocutor) and stealth (or ambient) abuse, also known as gaslighting. This is the fostering, propagation and enhancement of an atmosphere of fear, intimidation, instability, unpredictability and irritation. There are no acts of traceable explicit abuse, nor any manipulative settings of control.

Projective vs. Directional Abuse

Projective abuse is the outcome of the abuser's projection defence mechanism. Projection is when the abuser attributes to others feelings and traits and motives that he possesses but deems unacceptable, discomfiting, and ill-fitting. This way he disowns these discordant features and secures the right to criticize and chastise others for having or displaying them. Such abuse is often cathartic (see the next pair of categories).

Directional abuse is not the result of projection. It is a set of behaviours aimed at a target (the victim) for the purpose of humiliating, punishing, or manipulating her. Such abusive conduct is functional, geared towards securing a favoured and desired outcome.

Cathartic vs. Functional Abuse

While pair number above deals with the psychodynamic roots of the abuser's misbehaviour, the current pair of categories is concerned with its consequences. Some abusers behave the way they do because it alleviates their anxieties; enhances their inflated, grandiose self-image; or purges "impurities" and imperfections that they perceive either in the victim, or in the situation (e.g., in their marriage). Thus, such abuse is cathartic: it is aimed at making the abuser feel better. Projective abuse, for instance, is always cathartic.

The other reason to abuse someone is because the abuser wants to motivate his victim to do something, to feel in a certain way, or to refrain from committing an act. This is functional abuse in that it helps the abuser to adapt to his environment and operate in it, however dysfunctionally.

Pattern (or Structured) vs. Stochastic (or Random) Abuse

Some abusers heap abuse all the time on everyone around them: spouse, children, neighbours, friends, bosses, colleagues, authority figures, and underlings. Abusive conduct is the only way they know how to react to a world which they perceive to be hostile and exploitative. Their behaviours are "hard-wired", rigid, ritualistic, and structured.

Other abusers are less predictable. They are explosive and impulsive. They have a problem with managing their anger. They respond with temper tantrums to narcissistic injuries and real and imaginary slights (ideas of reference). These abusers appear to strike "out of the blue", in a chaotic and random manner.

Monovalent vs. Polyvalent Abuse

The monovalent abuser abuses only one party, repeatedly, viciously, and thoroughly. Such abusers perpetrate their acts in well-defined locations or frameworks (e.g., at home, or in the workplace). They take great care to hide their hideous exploits and present a socially-acceptable face (or, rather, facade) in public. They are driven by the need to annihilate the object of their maltreatment, or the source of their frustration and pathological envy.

In contrast, the polyvalent abuser casts his net wide and far and does not "discriminate" in choosing his prey. He is an "equal opportunity abuser" with multiple victims, who, often, have little in common. He is rarely concerned with appearances and regards himself above the Law. He holds everyone - and especially authority figures - in contempt. He is usually antisocial (psychopathic) and narcissistic.

Characteristic (Personal Style) vs. Atypical Abuse

Abuse amounts to the personal style of most pattern, or structured abusers. Demeaning, injurious, humiliating, and offensive behaviour is their modus operandi, their reflexive reaction to stimuli, and their credo. Stochastic, or random abusers, act normatively and "normally" most of the time. Their abusive conduct is an aberration, a deviation, and perceived by their nearest and dearest to be atypical and even shocking.

Normative vs. Deviant Abuse

We all inflict abuse on others from time to time. Some abusive reactions are within the social norms and not considered to be indicative or a personal pathology, or of a socio-cultural anomie. In certain circumstances, abuse as a reaction is called for and deemed healthy and socially-commendable.

Still, the vast majority of abusive behaviours should be regarded as deviant, pathological, antisocial, and perverse.

It is important to distinguish between normative and deviant abuse. A total lack of aggression is as unhealthy as a surfeit. The cultural context is critical in assessing when someone crosses the line and becomes an abuser.

Return

CHAPTER THREE

Coping with Your Abuser

Question: How to cope with the abuser?

Answer: Sometimes it looks hopeless. Abusers are ruthless, immoral, sadistic, calculated, cunning, persuasive, deceitful - in short, they appear to be invincible. They easily sway the system in their favour.

Here is a list of escalating countermeasures. They represent the distilled experience of thousands of victims of abuse. They may help you cope with abuse and overcome it.

Not included are legal or medical steps. Consult an attorney, an accountant, a therapist, or a psychiatrist, where appropriate.

Many abusers are narcissists or psychopaths.

First, you must decide:

Do you want to stay with him - or terminate the relationship?

[If you want to leave him and you have common children - Click here]

I Want to Stay with Him

Five Don't Do's - How to Avoid the Wrath of the Narcissist

- Never disagree with the narcissist or contradict him;
- Never offer him any intimacy;
- Look awed by whatever attribute matters to him (for instance: by his professional achievements or by his good looks, or by his success with women and so on);
- Never remind him of life out there and if you do, connect it somehow to his sense of grandiosity;
- Do not make any comment, which might directly or indirectly impinge on his self-image, omnipotence, omniscience, judgement, skills, capabilities, professional record, or even omnipresence.

The Ten Do's - How to Make Your Narcissist Dependent on You If You Insist on Staying with Him

- Listen attentively to everything the narcissist says and agree with it all. Don't believe a word of it but let it slide as if everything is just fine, business as usual;
- Personally offer something absolutely unique to the narcissist which they cannot obtain anywhere else. Also be prepared to line up future Sources of Primary Narcissistic Supply for your narcissist because you will not be *it* for very long, if at all. If you take over the procuring function for the narcissist, they become that much more dependent on you;
- Be endlessly patient and go way out of your way to be accommodating, thus keeping the Narcissistic Supply flowing liberally, and keeping the peace;
- Be endlessly giving. This one may not be attractive to you, but it is a take it or leave it proposition;
- Be absolutely emotionally and financially independent of the narcissist. Take what you need: the excitement and engulfment and refuse to get upset or hurt when the narcissist does or says something dumb, rude, or insensitive. Yelling back works really well but should be reserved for special occasions when you fear your narcissist may be on the verge of leaving you; the silent treatment is better as an ordinary response, but it must be carried out without any emotional content, more with the air of boredom and "I'll talk to you later, when I am good and ready, and when you are behaving in a more reasonable fashion". Treat your narcissist as you would a child;
- If your narcissist is cerebral and *not* interested in having much sex – then give yourself ample permission to have "hidden" sex with other people. Your Cerebral Narcissist will not be indifferent to infidelity so discretion and secrecy is of paramount importance;
- If your narcissist is somatic and you don't mind, join in on group sex encounters but make sure that you choose properly for your narcissist. If you do mind – leave him. Somatic Narcissists are sex addicts and incurably unfaithful;
- If you are a "fixer", then focus on fixing situations, preferably before they become "situations". Don't for one moment delude yourself that you can *fix* the narcissist – it simply will not happen;
- If there is any fixing that can be done, it is to help your narcissist become aware of their condition, with no negative implications or accusations in the process at all. It is like living with a

physically handicapped person and being able to discuss, calmly, unemotionally, what the limitations and benefits of the handicap are and how the two of you can work with these factors, rather than trying to change them;

- *Finally*, and most important of all: *Know Yourself*. What are you getting from the relationship? Are you actually a masochist? A codependent? Why is this relationship attractive and interesting? Define for yourself what good and beneficial things you believe you are receiving in this relationship. Define the things that you find harmful *to you*. Develop strategies to minimize the harm to yourself. Don't expect that you will cognitively be able to reason with the narcissist to change who he is. You may have some limited success in getting your narcissist to tone down on the really harmful behaviours *that affect you* - but this can only be accomplished in a very trusting, frank and open relationship.

Insist on Your Boundaries - Resist Abuse

- Refuse to accept abusive behaviour. Demand reasonably predictable and rational actions and reactions. Insist on respect for your boundaries, predilections, preferences, and priorities;
- Demand a just and proportional treatment. Reject or ignore unjust and capricious behaviour;
- If you are up to the inevitable confrontation, react in kind. Let him taste some of his own medicine;
- Never show your abuser that you are afraid of him. Do not negotiate with bullies. They are insatiable. Do not succumb to blackmail;
- If things get rough- disengage, involve law enforcement officers, friends and colleagues, or threaten him (legally);
- Do not keep your abuse a secret. Secrecy is the abuser's weapon;
- Never give him a second chance. React with your full arsenal to the first transgression;
- Be guarded. Don't be too forthcoming in a first or casual meeting. Gather intelligence;
- Be yourself. Don't misrepresent your wishes, boundaries, preferences, priorities, and red lines;
- Do not behave inconsistently. Do not go back on your word. Be firm and resolute;
- Stay away from such quagmires. Scrutinize every offer and suggestion, no matter how innocuous;
- Prepare backup plans. Keep others informed of your whereabouts and apprised of your situation;

- Be vigilant and doubting. Do not be gullible and suggestible. Better safe than sorry;
- Often the abuser's proxies are unaware of their role. Expose him. Inform them. Demonstrate to them how they are being abused, misused, and plain used by the abuser;
- Trap your abuser. Treat him as he treats you. Involve others. Bring it into the open. Nothing like sunshine to disinfest abuse.

Mirror His Behaviour

Mirror the narcissist's actions and repeat his words. If he threatens - threaten back and credibly try to use the same language and content. If he leaves the house - do the same, disappear on him. If he is suspicious - act suspicious. Be critical, denigrating, humiliating, and go down to his level - because that's the only way to penetrate his thick defences. Faced with his mirror image, the narcissist always recoils.

You will find that when you mirror the narcissist constantly and consistently, he becomes obsequious and tries to make amends, moving from one (cold and bitter, cynical and misanthropic, cruel and sadistic) pole to another (warm, even "loving", emotional, fuzzy, engulfing, maudlin, and saccharine).

Frighten Him

Narcissists live in a state of constant rage, repressed aggression, envy, and hatred. They firmly believe that everyone else is precisely like them. As a result, they are paranoid, scared, unpredictable, suspicious, and labile. Frightening the narcissist is a powerful behaviour modification tool. When sufficiently deterred, the narcissist promptly disengages, gives up everything he had fought for and sometimes makes amends.

To act effectively, one has to identify the vulnerabilities and susceptibilities of the narcissist and strike repeated, escalating blows at them until the narcissist lets go and vanishes.

Example: If a narcissist has a secret, one should use this fact to threaten him. One should drop cryptic hints that there are mysterious witnesses to the events and recently revealed evidence. The narcissist has a very vivid imagination. Let it do the rest.

The narcissist may have been involved in tax evasion, in malpractice, in child abuse, in infidelity - there are so many possibilities, which offer a rich vein of attack. If these insinuations are done cleverly, noncommittally, gradually, legally, and incrementally, the narcissist crumbles, disengages and disappears.

He lowers his profile thoroughly in the hope of avoiding hurt and pain.

Many narcissists have been known to disown and abandon a whole Pathological Narcissistic Space in response to a well-focused campaign by their victims. Thus, the narcissist may leave town, change his job, abandon a field of professional interest, and avoid friends and acquaintances only to relieve the unrelenting pressure exerted on him by his victims.

To reiterate: most of the drama takes place in the paranoid mind of the narcissist. His imagination runs amok. He finds himself snarled by horrifying scenarios, pursued by the vilest "certainties". The narcissist is his own worst persecutor and prosecutor.

You don't have to do much except utter a vague reference, make an ominous allusion, and delineate a possible turn of events. The narcissist will do the rest for you. He is like a small child in the dark, generating the very monsters that paralyse him with all-consuming fear.

Needless to add that all these activities have to be pursued legally, preferably through the good services of law offices and in broad daylight. Done the wrong way, they might constitute extortion or blackmail, harassment and a host of other criminal offences.

Lure Him

Another way to neutralize a vindictive narcissist is to offer him continued <u>Narcissistic Supply</u> until the war is over and won by you. Dazzled by the drug of Narcissistic Supply, the narcissist immediately becomes tamed, forgets his vindictiveness and triumphantly claims his "property" and "territory".

Under the influence of Narcissistic Supply, the narcissist is unable to tell when he is being <u>manipulated</u>. He is blind, dumb and deaf. You can make a narcissist do anything by offering, withholding, or threatening to withhold Narcissistic Supply (adulation, admiration, attention, sex, awe, subservience, etc.).

Play on His Fear of Abandonment

The threat to abandon need not be explicit or conditional ("If you don't do something or if you do it, I will dump you"). It is sufficient to <u>confront</u> the narcissist, to completely ignore him, to insist on respect for one's boundaries and wishes, or to shout back at him. The narcissist takes these signs of personal autonomy to be harbingers of impending separation and reacts with anxiety.

The narcissist is a living emotional pendulum. If he gets too close to someone emotionally, if he becomes intimate with someone, he fears ultimate and inevitable abandonment. He, thus, immediately distances himself, acts cruelly and brings about the very abandonment that he fears in the first place. This is called the Approach-Avoidance Repetition Complex.

In this paradox lies the key to coping with the narcissist. If, for instance, he is having a rage attack – rage back. This will provoke in him fears of being abandoned and calm him down instantaneously (and eerily).

Manipulate Him

By playing on the narcissist's grandiosity and paranoia, it is possible to deceive and manipulate him effortlessly. Just offer him Narcissistic Supply – admiration, affirmation, adulation – and he is yours. Harp on his insecurities and his persecutory delusions – and he is likely to trust only you and cling to you for dear life. But be careful not to overdo it!

When asked how is the narcissist likely to react to continued mistreatment, I wrote this in one of my Pathological Narcissism FAQs:

"The initial reaction of the narcissist to a perceived humiliation is a conscious rejection of the humiliating input. The narcissist tries to ignore it, talk it out of existence, or belittle its importance, for instance by devaluing its sources. If this crude mechanism of cognitive dissonance fails, the narcissist resorts to denial and repression of the humiliating material. He 'forgets' all about it and, when reminded of it, denies it.

But these are usually merely stopgap measures. The disturbing data are bound to impinge on the narcissist's tormented consciousness. Once aware of their re-emergence, the narcissist uses fantasy to counteract and counterbalance it. He imagines all the horrible things that he would do to the sources of his frustration.

It is through fantasy that the narcissist seeks to redeem his pride and dignity and to re-establish his damaged sense of uniqueness and grandiosity. Paradoxically, the narcissist does not mind being humiliated if this were to make him more unique or draw more attention to his person.

For instance: if the degree of injustice involved in the process of humiliation is unprecedented, or if the humiliating acts or words place the narcissist in a unique position, or if they transform him into a public figure, the narcissist tries to encourage such behaviours and to elicit them from others.

In this case, he fantasizes how he would defiantly demean and debase his opponents by forcing them to behave even more barbarously than before, so that their unjust conduct is universally recognized as such and condemned and the narcissist is publicly vindicated and his self-respect restored. In short: martyrdom is as good a method of obtaining <u>Narcissist Supply</u> as any.

Fantasy, though, has its limitations and, once reached, the narcissist is likely to experience waves of self-loathing and self-hatred, the bitter fruits of his helplessness and of the realization of the depths of his dependence on Narcissistic Supply. These feelings culminate in severe self-directed aggression: depression, <u>destructive, self-defeating behaviours</u> or suicidal ideation.

These self-negating reactions, inevitably and naturally, terrify the narcissist. He tries to project them on to his environment. He may decompensate by developing obsessive-compulsive traits or by going through a psychotic microepisode.

At this stage, the narcissist is suddenly besieged by disturbing, uncontrollable violent thoughts. He develops ritualistic reactions to them: a sequence of motions, obsessive counter-thoughts, or an act. Or he might visualize his aggression, or experience auditory hallucinations. Humiliation affects the narcissist this deeply and profoundly.

The process is entirely reversible once Narcissistic Supply is resumed. Almost immediately, the narcissist swings from one pole to another, from being humiliated to being elated; from being put down to being reinstated; from being at the bottom of his own, imagined, pit to occupying the top of his own, equally imagined, Everest."

I Can't Take It Any Longer - I Have Decided to Leave Him

Fight Him in Court

Here are a few of the things the narcissist finds devastating, especially in a court of law, for instance during a deposition:

- Any statement or fact, which seems to contradict his inflated perception of his grandiose self. Any criticism, disagreement, exposure of fake achievements, belittling of "talents and skills" which the narcissist fantasizes that he possesses, any hint that he is subordinated, subjugated, controlled, owned or dependent upon a third party. Any description of the narcissist as average and common, indistinguishable from many others. Any hint that the narcissist is weak, needy, dependent, deficient, slow, not intelligent, naive, gullible, susceptible, not in the know, manipulated, a victim;
- The narcissist is likely to react with rage to all these and, in an effort to re-establish his fantastic grandiosity, he is likely to

expose facts and stratagems he had no conscious intention of exposing;

- The narcissist reacts with narcissistic rage, hatred, aggression, or violence to an infringement of what he perceives to be his entitlement. Any insinuation, hint, intimation, or direct declaration that the narcissist is not special at all, that he is average, common, not even sufficiently idiosyncratic to warrant a fleeting interest will inflame the narcissist;
- Tell the narcissist that he does not deserve the best treatment, that his needs are not everyone's priority, that he is boring, that his needs can be catered to by an average practitioner (medical doctor, accountant, lawyer, psychiatrist), that he and his motives are transparent and can be easily gauged, that he will do what he is told, that his temper tantrums will not be tolerated, that no special concessions will be made to accommodate his inflated sense of self, that he is subject to court procedures, etc. – and the narcissist will lose control;
- Contradict, expose, humiliate, and berate the narcissist ("You are not as intelligent as you think you are", "Who is really behind all this? It takes sophistication which you don't seem to have", "So, you have no formal education", "You are (mistake his age, make him much older) ... sorry, you are ... old", "What did you do in your life? Did you study? Do you have a degree? Did you ever establish or run a business? Would you define yourself as a success?", "Would your children share your view that you are a good father?", "You were last seen with a Ms. ... who is (suppressed grin) a *cleaning lady* (in demeaning disbelief)";
- Be equipped with absolutely unequivocal, first rate, thoroughly authenticated and vouched for information.

If You Have Common Children

I described in The Guilt of the Abused: Pathologizing the Victim how the system is biased and titled against the victim.

Regrettably, mental health professionals and practitioners – marital and couple therapists, counsellors – are conditioned, by years of indoctrinating and dogmatic education, to respond favourably to specific verbal cues.

The paradigm is that abuse is rarely one sided – in other words, that it is invariably "triggered" either by the victim or by the mental health problems of the abuser. Another common lie is that all mental health problems can be successfully treated one way (talk therapy) or another (medication).

This shifts the responsibility from the offender to his prey. The abused must have done something to bring about their own maltreatment – or simply were emotionally "unavailable" to help the abuser with his problems. Healing is guaranteed if only the victim were willing to participate in a treatment plan and communicate with the abuser. So goes the orthodoxy.

Refusal to do so – in other words, refusal to risk further abuse – is harshly judged by the therapist. The victim is labelled uncooperative, resistant, or even abusive!

The key is, therefore, feigned acquiescence and collaboration with the therapist's scheme, acceptance of his/her interpretation of the events, and the use of key phrases such as: "I wish to communicate/work with (the abuser)", "trauma", "relationship", "healing process", "inner child", "the good of the children", "the importance of fathering", "significant other" and other psycho-babble. Learn the jargon, use it intelligently and you are bound to win the therapist's sympathy.

Above all – do not be assertive or aggressive, and do not overtly criticize the therapist or disagree with him/her.

I make the therapist sound like yet another potential abuser – because in many cases, he/she becomes one as they inadvertently collude with the abuser, invalidate the abuse experiences, and pathologize the victim.

Refuse All Contact

- Be sure to maintain as much contact with your abuser as the courts, counsellors, mediators, guardians, or law enforcement officials mandate;
- Do *not* contravene the decisions of the system. Work from the inside to change judgements, evaluations, or rulings – but *never* rebel against them or ignore them. You will only turn the system against you and your interests;
- But with the exception of the minimum mandated by the courts – decline any and all *gratuitous* contact with the abuser;
- Do not respond to his pleading, romantic, nostalgic, flattering, or threatening e-mail messages;
- Return all gifts he sends you;
- Refuse him entry to your premises. Do not even respond to the intercom;
- Do not talk to him on the phone. Hang up the minute you hear his voice while making clear to him, in a single, polite but firm, sentence, that you are determined not to talk to him;
- Do not answer his letters;

- Do not visit him on special occasions, or in emergencies;
- Do not respond to questions, requests, or pleas forwarded to you through third parties;
- Disconnect from third parties whom you know are spying on you at his behest;
- Do not discuss him with your children;
- Do not gossip about him;
- Do not ask him for anything, even if you are in dire need;
- When you are forced to meet him, do not discuss your personal affairs – or his;
- Relegate any inevitable contact with him – when and where possible – to professionals: your lawyer, or your accountant.

Return

CHAPTER FOUR

Avoiding Your Abuser

There is nothing special about the body language or behaviour patterns of the abuser. If your abuser is a narcissist, his pathology is evident on first sight (read "How to Recognize a Narcissist"). But not all abusers are narcissists. Regrettably, most victims find themselves trapped long before they have become aware of any warning sign.

Remember that abuse is a multifaceted phenomenon. It is a poisonous cocktail of control-freakery, conforming to social and cultural norms, and latent sadism. The abuser seeks to subjugate his victims and "look good" or "save face" in front of family and peers. Many abusers also enjoy inflicting pain on helpless victims.

But, even assuming that you want to stay with your abuser and to maintain the relationship, maltreatment can, to some extent, be avoided.

The Submissive Posture

Abusers react to the slightest provocation – real or imagined – with disproportionate wrath and, often, violence. It is important, therefore, never to openly and repeatedly disagree with your abuser or contradict him. If you do – your abuser is bound to walk away, but only after he has vilified and harmed you in every way he can.

Abusers feel threatened by real sharing and common decision-making. Never offer your abuser any intimacy – it is a sure way to turn him off and his aggression on. Abusers perceive intimacy as the prelude to manipulation ("What is she getting at? What does she really want? What is her hidden agenda?").

Abusers are narcissistic – so admire and adore them openly. But do not lie or exaggerate – this will be perceived as cunning and will provoke your abuser to feats of paranoia and jealousy. Look awed by whatever matters to him (for instance: by his professional achievements or by his good looks, or even by his success with other women).

The abuser tries to transform his personal space into the exact opposite of his real life. At home, he is the master of a fantasy of perfection and harmony and the undisputed recipient of adulation and obeisance. Any reminder that, in reality, his life is a drab dead end, that he is a failure, or a tyrant, or a swindler, or a wannabe, sometimes hated by his own oppressed family – is likely to be met with unbridled hostility.

Never remind him of life out there and if you do, connect it somehow to his sense of grandiosity. Reassure him of the permanence of your obedient and self-sacrificial love for him. Do not make any comment, which might directly or indirectly impinge on his self-image, omnipotence, judgement, omniscience, skills, capabilities, professional record, or even omnipresence.

Listen attentively to his words and never disagree, or contradict him or offer your point of view. You are there to witness the abuser's train of thought – not to derail it with reminders of your separate existence. Be saintly patient and accommodating and endlessly giving with nothing in return. Never let your energy be depleted or your guard down.

Your abuser is likely to be provoked to extremes by signs of your personal autonomy. Conceal your thoughts and plans, make no overt choices and express no preferences, never mention your emotions, needs, earnings, wages, profits, or trust money. Tell him how much you rely on him to reach the right decisions for both of you. Play dumb - but not too dumb, or it may be provoke his suspicions. It is a thin line between pleasing the abuser and rendering him a raving paranoid.

Never give your abuser cause to doubt or suspect you. Surrender all control to him, deny yourself access to property and funds, don't socialize, drop all your friends and hobbies, quit your job and your studies, and confine yourself to your abode. Your abuser is bound to be virulently jealous and suspect illicit liaisons between you and the least likely persons, your family included. He envies the attention you give to others, even to your common children. Place him on a pedestal and make sure he notices how you ignore, spurn, and neglect everyone else.

To your abuser, you are an object, no matter how ostensibly revered and cherished. Hence the battering. He monopolizes your time and your mind. He makes for you even the minutest choices: what to wear, what to cook for dinner, when to go out and with whom. In extreme cases, he regards even your body as his to share with others, if he sees fit.

It is an onerous existence, consistently tiptoeing on eggshells. Neither is it invariably successful. The submissive posture delays the more egregious manifestations of abuse but cannot prevent them altogether. Choosing to live with an abuser is like opting to share a cage with a predator. No matter how domesticated, Nature is bound to prevail. You are more likely than not to end up as the abuser's next meal.

Unless, that is, you adopt the Conflictive Posture.

The Conflictive Posture

Contrary to its name, the conflictive posture is actually about avoiding conflict by minimizing contact and insisting on boundaries. It is about refusal to accept abusive behaviour by demanding reasonably predictable and rational actions and reactions. It is about respect for you and for your predilections, preferences, emotions, needs, and priorities.

A healthy relationship requires justice and proportionality. Reject or ignore unjust and capricious behaviour. Conflicts are inevitable even in the most loving and mature bonds – but the rules of engagement are different in an abusive liaison. There, you must react in kind and let him taste some of his own medicine.

Abusers are predators, attuned to the subtlest emotional cues of their prey. Never show your abuser that you are afraid or that you are less than resolute. The willingness to negotiate is perceived as a weakness by bullies. Violent offenders are insatiable. Do not succumb to blackmail or emotional extortion – once you start compromising, you won't see the end of it.

The abuser creates a "shared psychosis" (folie a deux) with his victim, an overwhelming feeling of "the two of us against the whole world". Don't buy into it. Feel free to threaten him (with legal measures), to disengage if things get rough- or to involve law enforcement officers, friends, neighbours, and colleagues.

Here are a few counterintuitive guidelines:

The abused feel ashamed, somehow responsible, guilty, and blameworthy for their maltreatment. The abuser is adept at instilling these erroneous notions in his victims ("Look what you made me do!"). So, above all, do not keep your abuse a secret. Secrecy is the abuser's weapon. Share your story with friends, colleagues, neighbours, social workers, the police, the media, your minister, and anyone else who will listen.

Don't make excuses for him. Don't try to understand him. Do not empathize with him - he, surely, does not empathize with you. He has no mercy on you – you, in return, do not harbour misplaced pity for him. Never give him a second chance. React with your full arsenal to the first transgression. Teach him a lesson he is unlikely to forget. Make him go elsewhere for his sadistic pursuits or to offload his frustrations.

Often the abuser's proxies are unaware of their role. Expose him. Inform them. Demonstrate to them how they are being abused, misused, and plain used by the abuser. Trap your abuser. Treat him as he treats you. Involve others. Bring it into the open. Nothing like sunshine to disinfest abuse.

There are a few techniques which work wonders with abusers. Some psychologists recommend to treat and repeat offenders as one would toddlers. The abuser is, indeed, an immature brat – though a dangerous one, endowed as he is with the privileges and capabilities of an adult. Sometimes ignoring his temper tantrums until it is over is a wise policy. But not very often – and, definitely not as a rule.

[See the previous chapter]

Return

CHAPTER FIVE

Reconditioning the Abuser

Question: Can abusers be "reconditioned"? Can they be "educated" or "persuaded" not to abuse?

Answer: Tackling each of these three elements separately and in conjunction sometimes serves to ameliorate abusive behaviour.

The abuser's need to control his environment is compulsive and motivated by fear of inevitable and painful loss. It has, therefore, emotional roots. The abuser's past experiences – especially in early childhood and adolescence – taught him to expect injurious relationships, arbitrary or capricious treatment, sadistic interactions, unpredictable or inconsistent behaviours, and their culmination – indifferent and sudden abandonment.

About half of all abusers are products of abuse – they have either endured or witnessed it. As there are many forms of past mistreatment – there are myriad shades of prospective abuse. Some abusers have been treated by Primary Objects (parents or caregivers) as instruments of gratification, objects, or mere extensions. They were loved on condition that they satisfied the wishes, dreams, and (often unrealistic) expectations of the parent. Others were smothered and doted upon, crushed under overweening, spoiling, or overbearing caregivers. Yet others were cruelly beaten, sexually molested, or constantly and publicly humiliated.

Such emotional wounds are not uncommon in therapeutic settings. They can be – and are – effectively treated, though the process is sometimes long and arduous, hampered by the abuser's resistance to authority and narcissism.

Some offenders abuse so as to conform to the norms of their society and culture and, thus, be "accepted" by peers and family. It is easier and more palatable to abuse one's spouse and children in a patriarchal and misogynist society – than in a liberal and egalitarian one. That these factors are overwhelmingly important is evidenced by the precipitous decline in intimate partner violence in the United States in the last two decades. As higher education and mass communications became widespread, liberal and feminist strictures permeated all spheres of life. It was no longer "cool" to batter one's mate.

Some scholars say that the amount of abuse remained constant and that the shift was merely from violent to non-violent (verbal, emotional, and ambient) forms of mistreatment. But this is not supported by the evidence.

Any attempt to recondition the abuser and alter the abusive relationship entails a change of social and cultural milieu. Simple steps like relocating to a different neighbourhood, surrounded by a different ethnic group, acquiring a higher education, and enhancing the family's income – often do more to reduce abuse than years of therapy.

The really intractable abuser is the sadist, who derives pleasure from other people's fears, consternation, pain, and suffering. Barring the administering of numbing medication, little can be done to counter this powerful inducement to hurt others deliberately. Cognitive-behavioural Therapies and Transactional Treatment Modalities have been known to help. Even sadists are amenable to reason and self-interest. The pending risk of punishment and the fruits of well-observed contracts with evaluators, therapists, and family – sometimes do the job.

[Read what the victims can do to cope with their abusers – Coping with Your Abuser and Avoiding Your Abuser]

But how to get your abuser to see reason in the first place? How to obtain for him the help he needs – without involving law enforcement agencies, the authorities, or the courts? Any attempt to broach the subject of the abuser's mental problems frequently ends in harangues and worse. It is positively dangerous to mention the abuser's shortcomings or imperfections to his face.

Return

CHAPTER SIX

Reforming the Abuser

Points to Ponder

How to get your abuser to see reason in the first place? How to obtain for him the help he needs – without involving law enforcement agencies, the authorities, or the courts? Any attempt to broach the subject of the abuser's mental problems frequently ends in harangues and worse. It is positively dangerous to mention the abuser's shortcomings or imperfections to his face.

As I wrote <u>elsewhere</u>, *"Abuse is a multifaceted phenomenon. It is a poisonous cocktail of control-freakery, conforming to social and cultural norms, and latent sadism. The abuser seeks to subjugate his victims and 'look good' or 'save face' in front of family and peers. Many abusers also enjoy inflicting pain on helpless victims."*

Hence the complexity of trying to prevent or control the abuser's behaviour. His family, friends, peers, co-workers, and neighbours – normally, levers of social control and behaviour modification – condone his misbehaviour. The abuser seeks to conform to norms and standards prevalent in his milieu, even if only implicitly. He regards himself as normal, definitely not in need of therapeutic intervention.

Thus, the complaints of a victim are likely to be met with hostility and suspicion by the offender's parents or siblings, for instance. Instead of reining in the abusive conduct, they are likely to pathologize the victim ("she is a nutcase") or label her ("she is a whore or a bitch").

Nor is the victim of abuse likely to fare better in the hands of law enforcement agencies, the courts, counsellors, therapists, and guardians ad litem. The propensity of these institutions is to assume that the abused has a hidden agenda – to abscond with her husband's property, or to deny him custody or visitation rights. [Read more about it in The Guilt of the Abused: Pathologizing the Victim]

Abuse remains, therefore, the private preserve of the predator and his prey. It is up to them to write their own rules and to implement them. No outside intervention is forthcoming or effective. Indeed, the delineation of boundaries and reaching an agreement on co-existence are the first important steps towards minimizing abuse in your relationships. Such a compact must include a provision obliging your abuser to seek professional help for his mental health problems.

Personal boundaries are not negotiable, neither can they be determined from the outside. Your abusive bully should have no say in setting them or in upholding them. Only you decide when they have been breached, what constitutes a transgression, what is excusable and what not.

The abuser is constantly on the lookout for a weakening of your resolve. He is repeatedly testing your mettle and resilience. He pounces on any and every vulnerability, uncertainty, or hesitation. Don't give him these chances. Be decisive and know yourself: what do you really feel? What are your wishes and desires in the short and longer terms? What price are you willing to pay and what sacrifices are you ready to make in order to be you? What behaviours will you accept and where does your red line run?

Verbalize your emotions, needs, preferences, and choices without aggression but with assertiveness and determination. Some abusers – the narcissistic ones – are detached from reality. They avoid it actively and live in fantasies of everlasting and unconditional love. They refuse to accept the inevitable consequences of their own actions. It is up to you to correct these cognitive and emotional deficits. You may encounter opposition – even violence – but, in the long-run, facing reality pays.

Play it fair. Make a list – if need be, in writing – of do's and don'ts. Create a "tariff" of sanctions and rewards. Let him know what actions of his – or inaction on his part – will trigger a dissolution of the relationship. Be unambiguous and unequivocal about it. And mean what you say. Again, showing up for counselling must be a cardinal condition.

Yet, even these simple, non-threatening initial steps are likely to provoke your abusive partner. Abusers are narcissistic and possessed of alloplastic defences. More simply put, they feel superior, entitled, above any law and agreement, and innocent. Others – usually the victims – are to blame for the abusive conduct ("see what you made me do?").

How can one negotiate with such a person without incurring his wrath? What is the meaning of contracts "signed" with bullies? How can one motivate the abuser to keep his end of the bargain – for instance, to actually seek therapy and attend the sessions? And how efficacious is psychotherapy or counselling to start with?

Return

CHAPTER SEVEN

Contracting with Your Abuser

Points to Ponder

How can one negotiate with an abuser without incurring his wrath? What is the meaning of contracts "signed" with bullies? How can one motivate the abuser to keep his end of the bargain – for instance, to actually seek therapy and attend the sessions? And how efficacious is psychotherapy or counselling to start with?

It is useless to confront the abuser head on and to engage in power politics ("You are guilty or wrong, I am the victim and right", "My will should prevail", and so on). It is decidedly counterproductive and unhelpful and could lead to rage attacks and a deepening of the abuser's persecutory delusions, bred by his humiliation in the therapeutic setting. Better, at first, to co-opt the abuser's own prejudices and pathology by catering to his infantile emotional needs and complying with his wishes, complex rules and arbitrary rituals.

Here a practical guide how to drag your abuser into treatment and into a contract of mutual respect and cessation of hostilities (assuming, of course, you want to preserve the relationship):

1. Tell him that you love him and emphasize the exclusivity of your relationship by refraining, initially and during the therapy, from anxiety-provoking acts. Limiting your autonomy is a temporary sacrifice – under no circumstances make it a permanent feature of your relationship. Demonstrate to the abuser that his distrust of you is misplaced and undeserved and that one of the aims of the treatment regimen is to teach him to control and reduce his pathological and delusional jealousy.

2. Define areas of your common life that the abuser can safely – and without infringing on your independence – utterly control.

Abusers need to feel that they are in charge, sole decision-makers and arbiters.

3. Ask him to define – preferably in writing – what he expects from you and where he thinks that you or your "performance" are "deficient". Try to accommodate his reasonable demands and ignore the rest. Do not, at this stage, present a counter-list. This will come later. To move him to attend couple or marital therapy, tell him that you need his help to restore your relationship to its former warmth and intimacy. Admit to faults of your own which you want "fixed" so as to be a better mate. Appeal to his narcissism and self-image as the omnipotent and omniscient macho. Humour him for a while.

4. Involve your abuser, as much as you can, in your life. Take him to meet your family, ask him to join in with your friends, to visit your workplace, to help maintain your car (a symbol of your independence), to advise you on money matters and career steps. Do not hand over control to him over any of these areas – but get him to feel a part of your life and try to mitigate his envy and insecurity.

5. Encourage him to assume responsibility for the positive things in his life and in your relationship. Compliment the beneficial outcomes of his skills, talents, hard work, and attitude. Gradually, he will let go of his alloplastic defences – his tendency to blame every mistake of his, every failure, or mishap on others, or on the world at large.

6. Make him own up to his feelings by identifying them. Most abusers are divorced from their emotions. They seek to explain their inner turmoil by resorting to outside agents ("Look what you made me do" or "They provoked me"). They are unaware of their anger, envy, or aggression. Mirror your abuser gently and unobtrusively ("How do you feel about it?", "When I am angry I act the same", "Would you be happier if I didn't do it?").

7. Avoid the appearance – or the practice – of manipulating your abuser (except if you want to get rid of him). Abusers are very sensitive to control issues and they feel threatened, exploited, and ill-treated when manipulated. They invariably react with violence.

8. Treat your abuser as you would like him to behave towards you. Personal example is a powerful proselytizer. Don't act out of fear or subservience. Be sincere. Act out of love and conviction. Finally, your conduct is bound to infiltrate the abuser's defences.

9. React forcefully, unambiguously, and instantly to any use of force. Make clear where the boundary of civilized exchange lies. Punish him severely and mercilessly if he crosses it. Make known well in advance the rules of your relationship - rewards and sanctions included. Discipline him for verbal and emotional abuse as well – though less strenuously. Create a hierarchy of transgressions and a penal code to go with it.
   [Read these for further guidance: Coping with Your Abuser and The Guilt of the Abused: Pathologizing the Victim]

10. As the therapy continues and progress is evident, try to fray the rigid edges of your sex roles. Most abusers are very much into "me Tarzan, you Jane" gender-casting. Show him his feminine sides and make him proud of them. Gradually introduce him to your masculine traits, or skills – and make him proud of you.

This, essentially, is what good therapists do in trying to roll back or limit the offender's pathology.

From "Treatment Modalities and Therapies":

"Most therapists try to co-opt the narcissistic abuser's inflated ego (False Self) and defences. They compliment the narcissist, challenging him to prove his omnipotence by overcoming his disorder. They appeal to his quest for perfection, brilliance, and eternal love - and his paranoid tendencies - in an attempt to get rid of counterproductive, self-defeating, and dysfunctional behaviour patterns.

By stroking the narcissist's grandiosity, they hope to modify or counter cognitive deficits, thinking errors, and the narcissist's victim-stance. They contract with the narcissist to alter his conduct. Some even go to the extent of medicalizing the disorder, attributing it to a hereditary or biochemical origin and thus 'absolving' the narcissist from guilt and responsibility and freeing his mental resources to concentrate on the therapy."

But is therapy worth the effort? What is the success rate of various treatment modalities in modifying the abuser's conduct, let alone in "healing" or "curing" him?

Return

CHAPTER EIGHT

How to Cope with a Narcissist?

No one should feel responsible for the narcissist's predicament. To him, others hardly exist – so enmeshed he is in himself and in the resulting misery of this very self-preoccupation. Others are objects on which he projects his wrath, rage, suppressed and mutating aggression and, finally, ill disguised violence. How should his closest, nearest and dearest cope with his eccentric vagaries?

The short answer is by abandoning him or by threatening to abandon him.

The threat to abandon need not be explicit or conditional ("If you don't do something or if you do it – I will ditch you"). It is sufficient to confront the narcissist, to completely ignore him, to insist on respect for one's boundaries and wishes, or to shout back at him. The narcissist takes these signs of personal autonomy to be harbinger of impending separation and reacts with anxiety.

The narcissist is tamed by the very same weapons that he uses to subjugate others. The spectre of being abandoned looms large over everything else. In the narcissist's mind, every discordant note presages solitude and the resulting confrontation with his self.

The narcissist is a person who is irreparably traumatized by the behaviour of the most important people in his life: his parents, role models, or peers. By being capricious, arbitrary, and sadistically judgemental, they moulded him into an adult, who fervently and obsessively tries to recreate the trauma in order to, this time around, resolve it (repetition complex).

Thus, on the one hand, the narcissist feels that his freedom depends upon re-enacting these early experiences. On the other hand, he is terrified by this prospect. Realizing that he is doomed to go through the same traumas over and over again, the narcissist distances himself by using his aggression to alienate, to humiliate and in general, to be emotionally absent.

This behaviour brings about the very consequence that the narcissist so fears - abandonment. But, this way, at least, the narcissist is able to tell himself (and others) that *he* was the one who fostered the separation, that it was fully his choice and that he was not surprised. The truth is that, governed by his internal demons, the narcissist has no real choice. The dismal future of his relationships is preordained.

The narcissist is a binary person: the carrot is the stick in his case. If he gets too close to someone emotionally, he fears ultimate and inevitable abandonment. He, thus, distances himself, acts cruelly and brings about the very abandonment that he feared in the first place.

In this paradox lies the key to coping with the narcissist. If, for instance, he is having a rage attack - rage back. This will provoke in him fears of being abandoned and the resulting calm will be so total that it might seem eerie. Narcissists are known for these sudden tectonic shifts in mood and in behaviour.

Mirror the narcissist's actions and repeat his words. If he threatens - threaten back and credibly try to use the same language and content. If he leaves the house - leave it as well, disappear on him. If he is suspicious - act suspicious. Be critical, denigrating, humiliating, go down to his level - because that's the only way to penetrate his thick defences. Faced with his mirror image - the narcissist always recoils.

We must not forget that the narcissist behaves the way he does in order to engender and encourage abandonment. When mirrored, the narcissist dreads imminent and impending desertion, which is the inevitable result of his actions and words. This prospect so terrifies him that it induces in him an incredible alteration of conduct.

He instantly succumbs and obsequiously tries to make amends, moving from one (cold and bitter, cynical and misanthropic, cruel and sadistic) pole to another (warm, even loving, fuzzy, engulfing, emotional, maudlin, and saccharine).

The other coping strategy is to give up on him.

Dump him and go about reconstructing your own life. Very few people deserve the kind of investment that is an absolute prerequisite to life with a narcissist. To cope with a narcissist is a full time, energy and emotion-draining job, which reduces people around him to insecure nervous wrecks. Who deserves such a sacrifice?

No one, to my mind, not even the most brilliant, charming, breathtaking, suave narcissist. The glamour and trickery wear thin and underneath them a monster lurks which irreversibly and adversely influences the lives of those around it for the worse.

Narcissists are incorrigibly and notoriously difficult to change. Thus, trying to "modify" them is doomed to failure. You should either accept them as they are or avoid them altogether. If one accepts the narcissist as he is – one should cater to his needs. His needs are part of what he is. Would you have ignored a physical handicap? Would you not have assisted a quadriplegic? The narcissist is an emotional cripple. He needs constant adulation. He cannot help it. So, if one chooses to accept him – it is a package deal, all his needs included.

Return

CHAPTER NINE

How to Cope with Your Paranoid Ex

Your abusive ex is likely to cope with the pain and humiliation of separation by spreading lies, distortions, and half-truths about you and by proffering self-justifying interpretations of the events leading to the breakup. By targeting your closest, nearest, and dearest – your family, your children, boss, colleagues, co-workers, neighbours, and friends – your ex hopes to achieve two equally unrealistic goals:

1. To isolate you socially and force you to come running back to his waiting and "loving" arms; and
2. To communicate to you that he still "loves" you, is still interested in you and your affairs and that, no matter what, you are inseparable. He magnanimously is willing to forgive all the "horrible things" you did to him and revive the relationship (which, after all, had its good moments).

All abusers present with rigid and infantile (primitive) defence mechanisms: splitting, projection, Projective Identification, denial, intellectualization, and narcissism. But some abusers go further and decompensate by resorting to self-delusion. Unable to face the dismal failures that they are, they partially withdraw from reality.

How to cope with delusional, paranoid – and, therefore, dangerous – stalkers?

It may be difficult, but turn off your emotions. Abusers prey on other people's empathy, pity, altruism, nostalgia, and tendency to lend a helping hand. Some stalkers "punish" themselves – drink to excess, commit offences and get caught, abuse drugs, have accidents, fall prey to scams – in order to force their victims to pity them and get in touch.

The only viable coping strategy is to ignore your abusive ex. Take all necessary precautions to protect yourself and your family. Alert law enforcement agencies to any misbehaviour, violence, or harassment. File charges and have restraining orders issued. But, otherwise, avoid all gratuitous interactions.

[See above: Refuse All Contact]

Do not collude or collaborate in your ex's fantasies and delusions. You cannot buy his mercy or his goodwill – he has none. Do not support his notions, even indirectly, that he is brilliant, perfect, irresistibly handsome, destined for great things, entitled, powerful, wealthy, the centre of attention, etc. Abusers act on these misperceptions and try to coerce you into becoming an integral part of their charades.

Abuse is a criminal offence and, by definition, abusers are criminals: they lack empathy and compassion, have deficient social skills, disregard laws, norms, contracts, and morals. You can't negotiate with your abusive ex and you can't strike a bargain with him. You can't reform, cure, or recondition him. He is a threat to you, to your property, and to your dear ones. Treat him as such.

The most dangerous class of abusers is the paranoid-delusional. If your ex is one of these, he is likely to:

1. Believe that you still love him (erotomania). Interpret everything you do or say – even to third parties – as "hidden messages" addressed to him and professing your undying devotion (ideas of reference);
2. Confuse the physical with the emotional (regard sex as "proof" of love and be prone to rape you);
3. Blame the failure of the relationship on you or on others – social workers, your friends, your family, your children;
4. Seek to "remove" the obstacles to a "happy" and long relationship – sometimes by resorting to violence (kidnapping or murdering the sources of frustration);
5. Be very envious of your newfound autonomy and try to sabotage it by reasserting his control over you (for instance, break and enter into your house, leave intrusive messages on your answering machine, follow you around and monitor your home from a stationary car);
6. Harm you (and sometimes himself) in a fit of indignation (and to punish you) if he feels that no renewed relationship is possible;
7. Develop persecutory delusions. Perceive slights and insults where none are intended. Become convinced that he is the centre of a conspiracy to deny him (and you) happiness, to humiliate him, punish him, delude him, impoverish him, confine him physically or intellectually, censor him, impose on his time, force him to action (or to inaction), frighten him, coerce him,

surround and besiege him, change his mind, part with his values, victimise or even murder him, and so on.

The paranoid's conduct is unpredictable and there is no "typical scenario". But experience shows that you can minimise the danger to yourself and to your household by taking some simple steps.

Return

CHAPTER TEN

Avoiding Your Paranoid Ex

The paranoid's conduct is unpredictable and there is no "typical scenario". But experience shows that you can minimise the danger to yourself and to your household by taking some basic steps.

If at all possible, put as much physical distance as you can between yourself and the stalker. Change address, phone number, email accounts, cell phone number, enlist the kids in a new school, find a new job, get a new credit card, open a new bank account. Do not inform your paranoid ex about your whereabouts and your new life. You may have to make painful sacrifices, such as minimize contact with your family and friends.

Even with all these precautions, your abusive ex is likely to find you, furious that you have fled and evaded him, raging at your newfound existence, suspicious and resentful of your freedom and personal autonomy. <u>Violence</u> is more than likely. Unless deterred, paranoid former spouses tend to be harmful, even lethal.

Be prepared: alert your local law enforcement officers, check out your neighbourhood domestic violence shelter, consider owning a gun for self-defence (or, at the very least, a stun gun or mustard spray). Carry these with you at all times. Keep them close by and accessible even when you are asleep or in the bathroom.

Erotomanic stalking can last many years. Do not let down your guard even if you haven't heard from him. Stalkers leave traces. They tend, for instance, to "scout" the territory before they make their move. A typical stalker invades his or her victim's privacy a few times long before the crucial and injurious encounter.

Is your computer being tampered with? Is someone downloading your e-mail? Has anyone been to your house while you were away? Any signs of breaking and entering, missing things, atypical disorder (or too much order)? Is your post being delivered erratically, some of the envelopes opened and then sealed? Mysterious phone calls abruptly disconnected when you pick up? Your stalker must have dropped by and is monitoring you.

Notice any unusual pattern, any strange event, any weird occurrence. Someone is driving by your house morning and evening? A new "gardener" or maintenance man came by in your absence? Someone is making enquiries about you and your family? Maybe it's time to move on.

Teach your children to avoid your paranoid ex and to report to you immediately any contact he has made with them. Abusive bullies often strike where it hurts most - at one's kids. Explain the danger without being unduly alarming. Make a distinction between adults they can trust - and your abusive former spouse, whom they should avoid.

Ignore your gut reactions and impulses. Sometimes, the stress is so onerous and so infuriating that you feel like striking back at the stalker. Don't do it. Don't play his game. He is better at it than you are and is likely to defeat you. Instead, unleash the full force of the law whenever you get the chance to do so: restraining orders, spells in jail, and frequent visits from the police tend to check the abuser's violent and intrusive conduct.

The other behavioural extreme is equally futile and counterproductive. Do not try to buy peace by appeasing your abuser. Submissiveness and attempts to reason with him only whet the stalker's appetite. He regards both as contemptible weaknesses, vulnerabilities he can exploit. You cannot communicate with a paranoid because he is likely to distort everything you say to support his persecutory delusions, sense of entitlement, and grandiose fantasies. You cannot appeal to his emotions - he has none, at least not positive ones.

Remember: your abusive and paranoid former partner blames it all on you. As far as he is concerned, you recklessly and unscrupulously wrecked a wonderful thing you both had going. He is vengeful, seething, and prone to bouts of uncontrolled and extreme aggression. Don't listen to those who tell you to "take it easy". Hundreds of thousands of women paid with their lives for heeding this advice. Your paranoid stalker is inordinately dangerous - and, more likely than not, he is with you for a long time to come.

How long and how it all ends depends on a few factors.

Return

CHAPTER ELEVEN

Coping with Your Stalker

Abuse by proxy continues long after the relationship is officially over (at least as far as you are concerned). The majority of abusers get the message, however belatedly and reluctantly. Others – more vindictive and obsessed – continue to haunt their ex-spouses for years to come. These are the stalkers.

Most stalkers are what Zona (1993) and Geberth (1992) call "Simple Obsessional" or, as Mullen and Pathe put it (1999) – "Rejected". They stalk their prey as a way of maintaining the dissolved relationship (at least in their diseased minds). They seek to "punish" their quarry for refusing to collaborate in the charade and for resisting their unwanted and ominous attentions.

Such stalkers come from all walks of life and cut across social, racial, gender, and cultural barriers. They usually suffer from one or more (comorbid) personality disorders. They may have anger management or emotional problems and they usually abuse drugs or alcohol. Stalkers are typically lonely, violent, and intermittently unemployed – but they are rarely full fledged criminals.

Contrary to myths perpetrated by the mass media, studies show that most stalkers are men, have high IQ's, advanced degrees, and are middle aged (Meloy and Gothard, 1995; and Morrison, 2001).

Rejected stalkers are intrusive and inordinately persistent. They recognize no boundaries – personal or legal. They honour to "contracts" and they pursue their target for years. They interpret rejection as a sign of the victim's continued interest and obsession with them. They are, therefore, impossible to get rid of. Many of them are narcissists and, thus, lack empathy, feel omnipotent and immune to the consequences of their actions.

Even so, some stalkers are possessed of an uncanny ability to psychologically penetrate others. Often, this gift is abused and put at the service of their control freakery and sadism. Stalking – and the ability to "mete out justice" makes them feel powerful and vindicated. When arrested, they often act the victim and attribute their actions to self-defence and "righting wrongs".

Stalkers are emotionally labile and present with rigid and infantile (primitive) defence mechanisms: splitting, projection, projective identification, denial, intellectualization, and narcissism. They devalue and dehumanize their victims and thus "justify" the harassment or diminish it. From here, it is only one step to violent conduct. [This is the topic of our next chapter]

Additional reading:
Coping with Stalking and Stalkers

Zona M.A., Sharma K.K., and Lane J.: A Comparative Study of Erotomanic and Obsessional Subjects in a Forensic Sample, Journal of Forensic Sciences, July 1993, 38(4):894-903;

Vernon Geberth: Stalkers, Law and Order, October 1992, 40: 138-140;

Mullen P.E., Pathé M., Purcell R., and Stuart G.W.: Study of Stalkers, American Journal of Psychiatry, August 1999, 156(8):1244-9;

Meloy J.R., Gothard S.: Demographic and Clinical Comparison of Obsessional Followers and Offenders with Mental Disorders, American Journal of Psychiatry, February 1995, 152(2):258-63;

Morrison K.A.: Predicting Violent Behaviour in Stalkers - A Preliminary Investigation of Canadian Cases in Criminal Harassment, Journal of Forensic Sciences, November 2001, 46(6):1403-10.

Return

CHAPTER TWELVE

The Stalker as Antisocial Bully

Stalkers have narcissistic traits. Many of them suffer from <u>personality disorders</u>. The vindictive stalker is usually a psychopath (has Antisocial Personality Disorder). They all conform to the classic definition of a bully.

Before we proceed to delineate coping strategies, it is helpful to review the characteristics of each of these mental health problems and dysfunctional behaviours.

The Narcissistic Stalker

The dramatic and erotomaniac stalker is likely to show one or more of these narcissistic traits:

- Feels grandiose and self-important (e.g., exaggerates accomplishments, talents, *skills, contacts, and personality traits to the point of lying, demands* to be recognised as superior without commensurate achievements);
- Is obsessed with fantasies of unlimited success, *fame, fearsome* power or *omnipotence, unequalled* brilliance *(the Cerebral Narcissist), bodily* beauty *or sexual performance (the Somatic Narcissist),* or ideal, *everlasting, all-conquering* love *or passion*;
- Firmly convinced that he or she is unique and, being special, can only be understood by, *should only be treated by,* or associate with, other special or unique, or high-status people (or institutions);
- Requires excessive admiration, *adulation, attention and affirmation - or, failing that, wishes to be feared and to be notorious (Narcissistic Supply)*;
- Feels entitled. *Demands automatic and full compliance* with his or her unreasonable expectations for special and *favourable priority* treatment;

- Is "interpersonally exploitative", i.e., *uses* others to achieve his or her own ends;
- *Devoid* of empathy. Is *unable* or unwilling to identify with, *acknowledge, or accept* the feelings, needs, *preferences, priorities, and choices* of others;
- Constantly envious of others *and seeks to hurt or destroy the objects of his or her frustration. Suffers from persecutory (paranoid) delusions as he or she* believes that they feel the same about him or her *and are likely to act similarly*;
- Behaves arrogantly and haughtily. *Feels superior, omnipotent, omniscient, invincible, immune, "above the law", and omnipresent (magical thinking). Rages when frustrated, contradicted, or confronted* by people he or she considers inferior to him or her and unworthy.

The Antisocial (Psychopathic) Stalker

APD or AsPD was formerly called "psychopathy" or, more colloquially, "sociopathy". Some scholars, such as Robert Hare, still distinguish psychopathy from mere antisocial behaviour. The disorder appears in early adolescence but criminal behaviour and substance abuse often abate with age, usually by the fourth or fifth decade of life. It may have a genetic or hereditary determinant and afflicts mainly men. The diagnosis is controversial and regarded by some scholar as scientifically unfounded.

Psychopaths regard other people as objects to be manipulated and instruments of gratification and utility. They have no discernible conscience, are devoid of empathy and find it difficult to perceive other people's nonverbal cues, needs, emotions, and preferences. Consequently, the psychopath rejects other people's rights and his commensurate obligations. He is impulsive, reckless, irresponsible and unable to postpone gratification. He often rationalises his behaviour showing an utter absence of remorse for hurting or defrauding others.

Their (primitive) defence mechanisms include splitting (they view the world – and people in it – as "all good" or "all evil"), projection (attribute their own shortcomings unto others) and Projective Identification (force others to behave the way they expect them to).

The psychopath fails to comply with social norms. Hence the criminal acts, the deceitfulness and identity theft, the use of aliases, the constant lying, and the conning of even his nearest and dearest for gain or pleasure. Psychopaths are unreliable and do not honour their undertakings, obligations, contracts, and responsibilities. They rarely hold a job for long or repay their debts. They are vindictive, remorseless, ruthless, driven, dangerous, aggressive, violent, irritable, and, sometimes, prone to magical thinking. They seldom plan for the long and medium terms, believing themselves to be immune to the consequences of their own actions.

[Adapted from my Mental Health Dictionary]

The Stalker as a Bully

Bullies feel inadequate and compensates for it by being violent – verbally, psychologically, or physically. Some bullies suffer from personality and other mental health disorders. They feel entitled to special treatment, seek attention, lack empathy, are rageful and envious, and exploit and then discard their co-workers.

Bullies are insincere, haughty, unreliable, and lack empathy and sensitivity to the emotions, needs, and preferences of others whom they regard and treat as objects or instruments of gratification.

Bullies are ruthless, cold, and have alloplastic defences (and outside locus of control) – they blame others for their failures, defeats, or misfortunes. Bullies have low frustration and tolerance thresholds, get bored and anxious easily, are violently impatient, emotionally labile, unstable, erratic, and untrustworthy. They lack self-discipline, are egotistic, exploitative, rapacious, opportunistic, driven, reckless, and callous.

Bullies are emotionally immature and control freaks. They are consummate liars and deceivingly charming. Bullies dress, talk, and behave normally. Many of them are persuasive, manipulative, or even charismatic. They are socially adept, liked, and often fun to be around and the centre of attention. Only a prolonged and intensive interaction with them – sometimes as a victim – exposes their dysfunctions.

[Based on an entry I have written for the Open Site Encyclopaedia – Workplace Bullying]

Return

CHAPTER THIRTEEN

Coping with Stalking and Stalkers

A Typology of Stalkers

Stalkers are not made of one cloth. Some of them are psychopaths, others are schizoids, narcissists, paranoids, or an admixture of these mental health disorders. Stalkers harass their victims because they are lonely, or because it is fun (these are latent sadists), or because they can't help it (clinging or codependent behaviour), or for a myriad different reasons.

Clearly, coping techniques suited to one type of stalker may backfire or prove to be futile with another. The only denominator common to all bullying stalkers is their pent-up rage. The stalker is angry at his or her targets and hates them. He perceives his victims as unnecessarily and churlishly frustrating. The aim of stalking is to "educate" the victim and to punish her.

Hence the catch-22 of coping with stalkers:

The standard – and good – advice is to avoid all contact with your stalker, to ignore him, even as you take precautions. But being evaded only inflames the stalker's wrath and enhances his frustration. The more he feels sidelined and stonewalled, the more persistent he becomes, the more intrusive and the more aggressive.

It is essential, therefore, to first identify the type of abuser you are faced with:

1. *The Erotomaniac* - This kind of stalker believes that he is in love with you and that, regardless of overwhelming evidence to the contrary, the feeling is reciprocal (you are in love with him). He interprets everything you do (or refrain from doing) as coded messages confessing your eternal devotion to him and to your "relationship". Erotomaniacs are lonely, socially-inapt people. They may also be people with whom you have been involved romantically (e.g., your former spouse, a former boyfriend, a

one night stand) – or otherwise (for instance, colleagues or co-workers).

2. *The Narcissist* – Feels entitled to your time, attention, admiration, and resources. Interprets every rejection as an act of aggression which leads to a narcissistic injury. Reacts with sustained rage and vindictiveness. Can turn violent because he feels omnipotent and immune to the consequences of his actions.

3. *The Paranoid* - By far the most dangerous the lot. Lives in an inaccessible world of his own making. Cannot be reasoned with or cajoled. Thrives on threats, anxiety, and fear. Distorts every communication to feed his persecutory delusions.

4. *The Antisocial (Psychopath)* - Though ruthless and, typically, violent, the psychopath is a calculating machine, out to maximise his gratification and personal profit. Psychopaths lack empathy and may even be sadistic – but understand well and instantly the language of carrots and sticks.

The Erotomaniac

This kind of stalker believes that he is in love with you. To show his keen interest, he keeps calling you, dropping by, writing e-mails, doing unsolicited errands "on your behalf", talking to your friends, co-workers, and family, and, in general, making himself available at all times. The erotomaniac feels free to make for you legal, financial, and emotional decisions and to commit you without your express consent or even knowledge.

The erotomaniac intrudes on your privacy, does not respect your express wishes and personal boundaries and ignores your emotions, needs, and preferences. To him – or her – "love" means enmeshment and clinging coupled with an overpowering separation anxiety (fear of being abandoned). He or she may even force himself (or herself) upon you sexually.

Moreover, no amount of denials, chastising, threats, and even outright hostile actions will convince the erotomaniac that you are not in love with him. He knows better and will make you see the light as well. You are simply unaware of what is good for you, divorced as you are from your emotions. The erotomaniac determinedly sees it as his or her task to bring life and happiness into your dreary existence.

Thus, regardless of overwhelming evidence to the contrary, the erotomaniac is convinced that his or her feelings are reciprocated – in other words, that you are equally in love with him or her. The erotomanic stalker interprets everything you do (or refrain from doing) as coded messages confessing to and conveying your eternal devotion to him and to your "relationship".

Erotomaniacs are socially-inapt, awkward, schizoid, and suffer from a host of mood and anxiety disorders. They may also be people with whom you have been involved romantically (e.g., your former spouse, a former boyfriend, a one night stand) – or otherwise (for instance, colleagues or co-workers). They are driven by their all-consuming loneliness and all-pervasive fantasies.

Consequently, erotomaniacs react badly to any perceived rejection by their victims. They turn on a dime and become dangerously vindictive, out to destroy the source of their mounting frustration – you. When the "relationship" looks hopeless, many erotomaniacs turn to violence in a spree of self-destruction.

Best coping strategy

Ignore the erotomaniac. Do not communicate with him or even acknowledge his existence.

The erotomaniac clutches at straws and often suffers from ideas of reference. He tends to blow out of proportion every comment or gesture of his "loved one".

Avoid contact – do not talk to him, return his gifts unopened, refuse to discuss him with others, delete his correspondence.

Follow the behaviour tips – Refuse All Contact Policy.

The Narcissist

Feels entitled to your time, attention, admiration, and resources. Interprets every rejection as an act of aggression which leads to a narcissistic injury. Reacts with sustained rage and vindictiveness. Can turn violent because he feels omnipotent and immune to the consequences of his actions.

[Read about the Narcissistic Stalker in the previous chapter]

Best coping strategy

Make clear that you want no further contact with him and that this decision is not personal.

Be firm. Do not hesitate to inform him that you hold him responsible for his stalking, bullying, and harassment and that you will take all necessary steps to protect yourself.

Narcissists are cowards and easily intimidated. Luckily, they never get emotionally attached to their prey and so can move on with ease.

[See other coping strategies in chapter three]

The Paranoid

[Read chapter ten: Avoiding Your Paranoid Ex]

The <u>Antisocial (Psychopath)</u>

Stalking is a crime and stalkers are criminals. This simple truth is often ignored by mental health practitioners, by law enforcement agencies, and by the media. The horrid consequences of stalking are often underestimated and stalkers are mocked as eccentric and lonely weirdoes. Yet, stalking affects one fifth of all women and an unknown number of men – and often ends in violence and bloodshed.

A 1997 Review Paper titled "Stalking (Part I) An Overview of the Problem" (Karen M. Abrams, MD, FRCPC1, Gail Erlick Robinson, MD, DPsych, FRCPC2) define stalking thus:

"Stalking, or criminal harassment, is defined as the 'wilful, malicious, and repeated following or harassing of another person', usually requiring a 'credible threat of violence' against the victim or the victim's family (1). 'Harass' refers to wilful conduct directed at a person that seriously alarms, annoys, or distresses the person and which serves no legitimate purpose (2). Typically, the behaviour involves such things as loitering near the victim, approaching, making multiple phone calls, constantly surveilling, harassing the victim's employer or children, harming a pet, interfering with personal property, sabotaging dates, and sending threatening or sexually suggestive 'gifts' or letters. The harassment usually escalates, often beginning with phone calls that gradually become more threatening and aggressive in nature, and frequently ends in violent acts (3). In essence, the offender's behaviour is terrorizing, intimidating, and threatening, and restricts the freedom of and controls the victim.

In the US, there are individual state laws but no unified federal antistalking laws. Under the Criminal Code of Canada, it is a crime to knowingly or recklessly harass another person in any of the following ways: (1) by repeatedly following or communicating either directly or indirectly with that person or anyone known to them; (2) by watching where that person or anyone known to them resides, works, or happens to be; or (3) by engaging in any threatening conduct directed at that person or his or her family, if any of these cause the person to reasonably fear for his or her safety. In both the US and Canada, antistalking laws are in a state of flux."

Many criminals suffer from personality disorders – most prevalently, the Antisocial Personality Disorder, formerly known as "psychopathy". Comorbidity – a "cocktail" of mental health disorders – is frequent. Most stalkers abuse substances (alcohol, drugs) and are prone to violence or other forms of aggression.

[Read about the Antisocial (Psychopathic) Stalker in the previous chapter]

Many psychopaths are outright bullies. Michigan psychologist Donald B. Saunders distinguishes between three types of aggressors: "family-only", "generally violent" (most likely to suffer from APD), and the "emotionally volatile". In an interview to Psychology Today, he described the "generally violent" thus:

"Type 2 men – the generally violent – use violence outside the home as well as in it. Their violence is severe and tied to alcohol; they have high rates of arrest for drunk driving and violence. Most have been abused as children and have rigid attitudes about sex roles. These men, Saunders explains, are calculating; they have a history with the criminal justice system and know what they can get away with."

[Read about The Stalker as a Bully in the previous chapter]

Though ruthless and, typically, violent, the psychopath is a calculating machine, out to maximise his gratification and personal profit. Psychopaths lack empathy and may even be sadistic – but understand well and instantly the language of carrots and sticks.

Best coping strategy

- Convince your psychopath that messing with your life or with your nearest is going to cost him dearly;
- Do not threaten him. Simply, be unequivocal and firm about your desire to be left in peace and your intentions to involve the Law should he stalk, harass, or threaten you;
- Give him a choice between being left alone and becoming the target of multiple arrests, restraining orders, and worse;
- Take extreme precautions at all times and meet him accompanied by someone and in public places – and only if you have no other choice;
- Minimise contact and interact with him through professionals (lawyers, accountants, therapists, police officers, judges);
- Document every contact, every conversation, try to commit everything to writing. You may need it as evidence;
- Educate your children to be on their guard and to exercise caution and good judgement;
- Keep fully posted and updated your local law enforcement agencies, your friends, the media, and anyone else who would listen;
- Be careful with your personal information. Provide only the bare and necessary minimum. Remember: he has ways of finding out;
- Under no circumstances succumb to his romantic advances, accept his gifts, respond to personal communications, show

interest in his affairs, help him out, or send him messages directly or through third parties. Maintain the <u>No Contact</u> rule;
- Equally, do not seek revenge. Do not provoke him, "punish him", taunt him, disparage him, bad-mouth or gossip about him or your relationship.

<u>Return</u>

CHAPTER FOURTEEN

Getting Help

This article is meant to be a general guide to seeking and finding help. It does not contain addresses, contacts, and phone numbers. It is not specific to one state or country. Rather, it describes options and institutions which are common the world over. You should be the one to "fill in the blanks" and locate the relevant groups and agencies in your domicile.

Your first "fallback" option is *your family*. They are, in many cases (though by no means always) your natural allies. They can provide you with shelter, money, emotional support, and advice. Don't hesitate to call on them in times of need.

Your friends and, to a lesser extent, *your colleagues and neighbours* will usually lend you a sympathetic ear and will provide you with useful tips. Merely talking to them can not only ease the burden – but protect you from future abuse. Stalkers and paranoids thrive on secrecy and abhor public exposure.

Regrettably, resorting to the *legal system* – your next logical step – is bound to be a disappointing, disempowering, and invalidating experience. [I wrote about it extensively in chapter The Guilt of the Abused: Pathologizing the Victim]

A 1997 Review Paper titled "Stalking (Part II) Victims' Problems with the Legal System and Therapeutic Considerations" (Karen M. Abrams, MD, FRCPC1, Gail Erlick Robinson, MD, DPsych, FRCPC2) note:

"Law-enforcement insensitivity toward domestic violence has already been well documented. Police often feel that, as opposed to serious crimes such as murder, domestic issues are not an appropriate police responsibility; 'private' misconduct should not be subject to public intervention, and, because few cases result in successful prosecution, pursuing domestic violence complaints is

ultimately futile... This sense of futility, reinforced by the media and the courts, may be transmitted to the victim.

In cases involving ex-lovers, the police may have equal difficulty in being sympathetic to the issues involved. As in the case of Ms A, society often views stalking as a normal infatuation that will eventually resolve itself or as the actions of a rejected lover or lovesick individual, more to be empathised with than censured (2). Victims often report feeling that the police and society blame them for provoking harassment or making poor choices in relationships. Authorities may have particular difficulty understanding the woman who continues to have ambivalent feelings toward the offender...

In terms of the laws themselves, there is a history of ineffectiveness in dealing with crimes of stalking (1, 5). The nature of the offences themselves makes investigations and prosecution difficult, because surveillance and phone calls often have no witnesses. Barriers to victims using civil actions against stalkers include dangerous time delays and financial requirements. Temporary restraining orders or peace bonds have been used most commonly and are generally ineffective, partly because law-enforcement agencies have limited resources to enforce such measures. Even if caught, violators receive, at most, minimal jail time or minor monetary penalties. Sometimes the offender just waits out the short duration of the order. Persistent, obsessed stalkers are usually not deterred."

Still, it is crucial that you document the abuse and stalking and duly report them to the *police* and to your *building security*. If your stalker is in jail, you should report him to the *wardens* and to his *parole officer*. It is important to resort to the *courts* in order to obtain restraining, or cease and desist orders. Keep law enforcement officers and agencies fully posted. Don't hesitate to call upon them as often as you need to. It is their job. Hire a *security expert* if the threat is credible or imminent.

You are well advised to rely on *professional advice* throughout your prolonged and arduous disentanglement from your paranoid and stalking ex. Use attorneys, accountants, private detectives, and therapists to communicate with him. Consult your *lawyer* (or, if you can't afford one, apply for a pro bono lawyer provided by a civic association, or your state's legal aid). Ask him or her what are your rights, what kinds of legal redress you have, what safety precautions you should adopt – and what are the do's and don't do's of your situation.

Especially important is to choose the right *therapist* for you and for your children. Check whether he or she has any experience with victims of stalking and with the emotional effects of constant threat and surveillance (fear, humiliation, ambivalence, helplessness, paranoid ideation). Stalking is a traumatic process and you may need intervention to ameliorate the post traumatic stress effects it wreaks.

Join online and offline *groups and organizations for victims of abuse and stalking*. Peer support is critical. Helping others and sharing experiences and fears with other victims is a validating and empowering as well as a useful experience. Realizing that you are not alone, that you are not crazy, and that the whole situation is not your fault helps to restore your shattered self-esteem and puts things in perspective.

The *social services* in your area are geared to deal with battering and stalking. They likely run shelters for victims of domestic violence and abuse, for instance.

Return

CHAPTER FIFTEEN

Domestic Violence Shelters

Shelters are run, funded, and managed either by governments or by volunteer non-government organizations. According to a 1999 report published by the National Coalition Against Domestic Violence, there are well over 2000 groups involved in sheltering abused women and their off-spring.

Before you opt for moving with your children into a sheltered home or apartment, go through this check list.

1. It is important to make sure that the philosophy of the organisers of the shelters accords with your own. Some shelters, for instance, are run by feminist movements and strongly emphasise self-organization, co-operation, and empowerment through decision-making. Other shelters are supervised by the Church or other religious organizations and demand adherence to a religious agenda. Yet others cater to the needs of specific ethnic minorities or neighbourhoods.

2. Can you abide by the house rules? Are you a smoker? Some shelters are for non-smokers. What about boyfriends? Most shelters won't allow men on the premises. Do you require a special diet due to medical reasons? Is the shelter's kitchen equipped to deal with your needs?

3. Gather intelligence and be informed before you make your move. Talk to battered women who spent time in the shelter, to your social worker, to the organisers of the shelter. Check the local newspaper archive and visit the shelter at least twice: in daytime and at night.

4. How secure is the shelter? Does it allow visitation or any contact with your abusive spouse? Does the shelter have its own security personnel? How well is the shelter acquainted with domestic violence laws and how closely is it collaborating with courts,

evaluators, and law enforcement agencies? Is recidivism among abusers tracked and discouraged? Does the shelter have a good reputation among them? You wouldn't want to live in a shelter that is shunned by the police and the judicial system.

5. How does the shelter tackle the needs of infants, young children, and adolescents? What are the services and amenities it provides? What things should you bring with you when you make your exit – and what can you count on the shelter to make available? What should you pay for and what is free of charge? How well-staffed is the shelter? Is the shelter well-organised? Are the intake forms anonymous?

6. How accessible is the shelter to public transport, schooling, and to other community services?

7. Does the shelter have a batterer intervention program or workshop and a women's support group? In other words, does it provide counselling for abusers as well as ongoing succour for their victims? Are the programs run only by volunteers (laymen peers)? Are professionals involved in any of the activities and, if so, in what capacity (consultative, supervisory)?

   Additionally, does the shelter provide counselling for children, group and individual treatment modalities, education and play-therapy services, along with case management services?

   Is the shelter associated with outpatient services such vocational counselling and job training, outreach to high schools and the community, court advocacy, and mental health services or referrals?

8. Most important: don't forget that shelters are a temporary solution. These are transit areas and you are fully expected to move on. Not everyone is accepted. You are likely to be interviewed at length and screened for both your personal needs and compatibility with the shelter's guidelines. Is it really a crisis situation, are your life or health at risk – or are you merely looking to "get away from it all"? Even then, expect to be placed on a waiting list. Shelters are not vacation spots. They are in the serious business of defending the vulnerable.

When you move into a shelter, you must know in advance what your final destination is. Imagine and plan your life after the shelter. Do you intend to relocate? If so, would you need financial assistance? What about the children's education and friends? Can you find a job? Have everything sorted out. Only then, pack your things and leave your abuser.

Return

CHAPTER SIXTEEN

Planning and Executing Your Getaway

Do not leave unprepared. Study and execute every detail of your getaway. This is especially important if your partner is violent. Be sure to make a Safety Plan – how to get out of the house unnoticed and the indispensable minimum items that you should carry with you, even on a short notice.

Here are the recommendations of the Province of Alberta in Canada:

Long before you actually leave, copy all important documents and store them in a safe place. These include: identity cards, health care and social insurance or security Cards, driver's license/registration, credit cards and bank cards, other personal identification (including picture ID), birth certificate, immunization card for the children, custody order, personal chequebook, last banking statement, and mortgage papers. Make a list of all computer passwords and access codes (for instance: ATM PINs).

When you leave the house, take with you these copied documents as well as the following personal items: prescribed medication, personal hygiene products, glasses/contact lenses, money (borrow from family members, a neighbour, colleague, or friends, if you have to), several changes of clothing (don't forget night wear and underwear), heirlooms, jewellery, photo albums (pictures that you want to keep), craft, needle work, hobby work.

The situation is inevitably more complicated if you are fleeing with your children. In this case, be sure to bring with you their various medications, soother, bottles, favourite toy or blanket, and clothing (again: night wear, underwear). Older kids may carry their own clothes and school books.

Make a list of the following and have it on you at all times: addresses and phone numbers of domestic violence shelters, police stations, night courts, community social services, schools in the vicinity, major media, and address and phone and fax numbers of your lawyer and his attorneys. Secure a detailed public transportation map.

Your best bet is to apply to a shelter for a safe place to stay the first few days and nights. [Read more about Domestic Violence Shelters in the previous chapter]

If you can afford to, your next step should be to hire a divorce attorney and file for interim custody. Your divorce papers can be served much later. Your first concern is to keep the children with you safely and legally. Your husband is likely to claim that you have kidnapped them.

But your escape should be only the tip of a long period of meticulous preparations.

We already mentioned that you should make copies of all important documents [see above]. Don't escape from your predicament penniless! Secretly put aside cash for an Escape Fund. Your husband is likely to block your checking account and credit cards. Ask around where you can stay the first week. Will your family or friends accept you? Apply to a domestic violence shelter and wait to be accepted. Be sure to know where you are going!

Make extra sets of keys and documents. Bundle these up with some clothes and keep these "reserve troves" with friends and family. Put one such "trove" in a safety deposit box and give the key to someone you trust. Secure transportation for the day or night of escape. Agree on codes and signals with friends and family ("If I don't call you by 10 PM, something has gone wrong", "If I call you and say that Ron is home, call the police").

You should wait until he is gone and only then leave home. Avoid confrontation over your departure. It can end badly. Do not inform him of your plans. Make excuses to slip away in the days and months before you actually leave. Get him used to your absence.

Should you get the police involved?

Return

CHAPTER SEVENTEEN

Getting Law Enforcement Authorities And the Police Involved

If you want the nightmare to end, there is a rule of thumb which requires courage and determination to implement:

Involve the police whenever possible.

Report his crimes as soon as you can and make sure you retain a copy of your complaint. Your abuser counts on your fear of him and on your natural propensity to keep domestic problems a secret. Expose him to scrutiny and penalties. This will make him re-consider his actions next time around.

Physical assault is a criminal offence as are rape and, in some countries, stalking and marital rape. If you have been physically or sexually assaulted, go to the nearest hospital and document your injuries. Be sure to obtain copies of the admission form, the medical evaluation report, and of any photographs and exam results (X-rays, computerised tomography-CT, biopsies, and so on).

If your abusive intimate partner verbally threatens you, your nearest and dearest, or your property or pets – this is also criminal conduct. To the best of your ability, get him on tape or make him repeat his threats in the presence of witnesses. Then promptly file a complaint with the police.

If your abuser forces you to remain indoors, in isolation, he is committing an offence. Forced confinement or imprisonment is illegal. While so incarcerated, failing to provide you with vital necessities – such as air, water, medical aid, and food – is yet another criminal act.

Damage to property rendering it inoperative or useless – is mischief. It is punishable by law. Same goes for cruelty to animals (let alone children).

If your partner swindled you out of funds or committed fraud, theft, or perjury (by falsifying your signature on a checking or credit card account, for instance) – report him to the police. Financial abuse is as pernicious as the physical variety.

In most countries, the police must respond to your complaint. They cannot just file it away or suppress it. They must talk to you and to your partner separately and obtain written and signed statements from both parties. The police officer on the scene must inform you of your legal options. The officer in charge must also furnish you with a list of domestic violence shelters and other forms of help available in your community.

If you suspect that a member of your family is being abused, the police, in most countries, can obtain a warrant permitting entry into the premises to inspect the situation. They are also authorised to help the victim relocate (leave) and to assist her in any way, including by applying on her behalf and with her consent to the courts to obtain restraining and emergency protection orders. A breach of either of these orders may be an indictable criminal offence as well as a civil offence.

If you decide to pursue the matter and if there are reasonable grounds to do so, the police will likely lay charges against the offender and accuse your partner of assault. Actually, your consent is only a matter of formality and is not strictly required. The police can charge an offender on the basis of evidence only.

If the team on the scene refuses to lay charges, you have the right to talk to a senior police officer. If you cannot sway them to act, you can lay charges yourself by going to the court house and filing with a Justice of the Peace (JP). The JP must let you lay charges. It is your inalienable right.

You cannot withdraw charges laid by the police and you most probably will be subpoenaed to testify against the abuser.

Should you get the courts involved?

Return

CHAPTER EIGHTEEN

Getting the Courts Involved

Restraining Orders and Peace Bonds

If you want the nightmare to end, there is a rule of thumb which requires courage and determination to implement:

Involve the courts whenever possible.

In many countries, the first step is to obtain a restraining order from a civil court as part of your divorce or custody proceedings or as a stand-alone measure.

In some countries, the police applies to the court for an emergency protection order on your behalf. The difference between a protection order and a restraining order is that the former is obtained following an incident of domestic violence involving injury or damage to property, it is available immediately, granted at the police's request, and issued even outside court hours.

Many restraining orders are granted ex parte, without the knowledge or presence of your abusive partner, based solely on a signed and sworn affidavit submitted by you. A typical emergency restraining order forbids the offender from visiting certain locations such as the children's schools, your workplace, or your home. It is later reviewed. At the review you should produce evidence of the abuse and witnesses. If the emergency or temporary order upheld it is fixed for a period of time at the judge's discretion.

Always carry the restraining order with you and leave copies at your place of employment and at your children's day-care and schools. You will have to show it to the police if you want to get your abuser arrested when he violates its terms. Breach of the restraining order is a criminal offence.

The wording of the order is not uniform – and it is crucial. "The police shall arrest" is not the same as "The police may arrest" the offender if he ignores the conditions set forth in the order. Don't forget to ask the court to forbid him to contact you by phone and other electronic means. Seek a new restraining order if you had moved and your place of residence or your workplace or the children's day-care or school changed.

If the abuser has visitation rights with the children, these should be specified in the order. Include a provision allowing you to deny the visit if he is intoxicated. The order can be issued against your abuser's family and friends as well if they harass and stalk you.

A restraining order is no substitute for taking precautionary measures to safeguard yourself and your children. Abusers often ignore the court's strictures and taunt you all the same. The situation can easily escalate and get out of hand. Be prepared for such unpleasant and dangerous eventualities.

Avoid empty and unlit areas, carry relevant emergency numbers with you at all times, install a personalised alarm system, wear comfortable shoes and clothes to allow you to run if attacked. Trust your senses – if you feel that you are being followed, go to a public place (restaurant, department store, cinema). Learn by rote the transit routes of all public transport around your home and workplace and make special arrangement with the cab operator nearest to you. You may also wish to consider buying a weapon or, at least, a spray can.

If you were physically or sexually assaulted or if you are being stalked or harassed, keep records of the incidents and a list of witnesses. Never hesitate to lay charges against your abuser, his family and friends. See your charges through by testifying against the offenders. Try not to withdraw the charges even if you worked out your problems. Abusers learn the hard way and a spell in jail (or even a fine) is likely to guarantee your future safety.

Based on a criminal police file, the criminal court can also force your abuser (and his family and friends if they have been harassing you) to sign a peace bond in the presence of a judge. It is a pledge of good behaviour, often requiring your abuser to stay away from your home and place of work for a period of 3-12 months. Some peace bonds forbid the abuser from carrying weapons.

Have the peace bond with you at all times and leave copies at your children's day-care and schools and at your place of employment. You will have to show it to the police if you want to get your abuser arrested when he violates its terms. Breach of the peace bond is a criminal offence.

Do not meet your abuser or speak to him while the restraining order or peace bond are in effect. The courts are likely to take a very dim view of the fact that you yourself violated the terms of these instruments of law issued for your protection and at your request.

There are many additional remedies the courts can apply. They can force your abusive partner to surrender to you household's items and clothing, to grant you access to bank accounts and credit cards, to defray some costs, to pay alimony and child support, to submit to psychological counselling and evaluation, and to grant the police access to his home and workplace. Consult your family or divorce attorney as to what else can be done.

In theory, the courts are the victims' friends. The truth, however, is a lot more nuanced. If you are not represented, your chances to get protection and prevail (to have your day in court) are slim. The courts also show some institutional bias in favour of the abuser. Yet, despite these hurdles there is no substitute to getting the legal system to weigh in and restrain your abuser. Use it wisely and you will not regret it.

Return

CHAPTER NINETEEN

The Narcissist in Court

Points to Ponder

It is very easy to "break" a narcissist in court by revealing facts that contradict his inflated perception of his grandiose (False) Self; by criticizing and disagreeing with him; by exposing his fake achievements, belittling his self-imputed and fantasized "talents and skills"; by hinting that he is subordinated, subjugated, controlled, owned or dependent upon a third party; by describing the narcissist as average, common, indistinguishable from others; by implying that the narcissist is weak, needy, dependent, deficient, slow, not intelligent, naive, gullible, susceptible, not in the know, manipulated, a victim, an average person of mediocre accomplishments.

Question: How can I expose the lies of the narcissist in a court of law? He acts so convincing!

Answer: You should distinguish the factual pillar from the psychological pillar of any cross-examination of a narcissist or a deposition made by him.

It is essential to be equipped with absolutely unequivocal, first rate, thoroughly authenticated and vouched-for information. The reason is that narcissists are superhuman in their capacity to distort reality by offering highly "plausible" alternative scenarios, which fit most of the facts.

It is very easy to "break" a narcissist – even a well-trained and well-prepared one.

Here are a few of the things the narcissist finds devastating:

• Any statement or fact, which seems to contradict his inflated perception of his grandiose self;

- Any hint that he is subordinated to, subjugated to, controlled by, owned or dependent upon a third party;
- Any criticism, disagreement, exposure of fake achievements, belittling of "talents and skills", which the narcissist fantasizes that he possesses;
- Any description of the narcissist as average and common, indistinguishable from others;
- Any hint that the narcissist is weak, needy, dependent, deficient, slow, not intelligent, naive, gullible, susceptible, not in the know, manipulated, a victim, or an average person of mediocre accomplishments.

The narcissist is likely to react with rage to all these and, in an effort to re-establish his fantastic grandiosity, he is likely to expose facts and stratagems he has had no conscious intention of exposing.

The narcissist reacts indignantly, with wrath, hatred, aggression, or even overt violence to any infringement of what he perceives to be his natural entitlement.

Narcissists believe that they are so unique and that their lives are of such cosmic significance that others should defer to their needs and cater to their every whim without ado. The narcissist feels entitled to interact with or be treated (or questioned) only by unique individuals. He resents being doubted and "ridiculed".

Any insinuation or hint, intimation, or direct declaration that the narcissist is not special at all, that he is average, common, not even sufficiently idiosyncratic to warrant a fleeting interest inflame the narcissist. He holds himself to be omnipotent and omniscient.

Tell the narcissist that he does not deserve the best treatment; that his desires are not everyone's priority; that he is boring or ignorant; that his needs can be catered to by any common practitioner (medical doctor, accountant, lawyer, psychiatrist); that he and his motives are transparent and can be easily gauged; that he will do what he is told; that his temper tantrums will not be tolerated; that no special concessions will be made to accommodate his inflated sense of self; that he is subject to court procedures, etc. - and the narcissist will likely lose control.

The narcissist believes that he is the cleverest of them all and far above the madding crowd.

Contradict him often; expose his shortcomings; disagree with him and criticize his judgement; counter his self-aggrandizing self-imputed role or narrative; humiliate and berate him: "You are not as intelligent as you think you are"; "Who is really behind all this? It takes sophistication which you don't seem to posses"; "So, you have no formal education"; "You are (mistake his age, make him much older)"; "What did you do in your life? Did you study? Do you have an academic degree? Did you ever establish or run a business? Would you define yourself as a success?"; "Would your children share your view that you are a good father?"; "You were last seen with a certain Ms. ... who is (suppressed grin) a stripper (in demeaning disbelief)."

I know that many of these questions cannot be asked outright in a court of law. But you can insinuate them or hurl these sentences at him during the breaks, or inadvertently during the examination or deposition phase, etc. Narcissists hate innuendos even more than they detest direct attacks.

Return

CHAPTER TWENTY

The Guilt of the Abused
Pathologizing the Victim

It is telling that precious few psychology and psychopathology textbooks dedicate an entire chapter to abuse and violence. Even the most egregious manifestations – such as child sexual abuse – merit a fleeting mention, usually as a sub-chapter in a larger section dedicated to paraphilias or personality disorders.

Abusive behaviour did not make it into the diagnostic criteria of mental health disorders, nor were its psychodynamic, cultural and social roots explored in depth. As a result of this deficient education and lacking awareness, most law enforcement officers, judges, counsellors, guardians, and mediators are worryingly ignorant about the phenomenon.

Only 4% of hospital emergency room admissions of women in the United States are attributed by staff to domestic violence. The true figure, according to the FBI, is more like 50%. One in three murdered women was done in by her spouse, current or former.

The US Department of Justice pegs the number of spouses (mostly women) threatened with a deadly weapon at almost 2 million annually. Domestic violence erupts in a mind-boggling half of all American homes at least once a year. Nor are these isolated, "out of the blue", incidents.

Mistreatment and violence are part of an enduring pattern of maladaptive behaviour within the relationship and are sometimes coupled with substance abuse. Abusers are possessive, pathologically jealous, dependent, and, often, narcissistic. Invariably, both the abuser and his victim seek to conceal the abusive episodes and their aftermath from family, friends, neighbours, or colleagues.

This dismal state of things is an abuser's and stalker's paradise. This is especially true with psychological (verbal and emotional) abuse which leaves no visible marks and renders the victim incapable of coherence.

Still, there is no "typical" offender. Maltreatment crosses racial, cultural, social, and economic lines. This is because, until very recently, abuse has constituted normative, socially-acceptable, and, sometimes, condoned, behaviour. For the bulk of human history, women and children were considered no better than property.

Indeed, well into the 18th century, they still made it into lists of assets and liabilities of the household. Early legislation in America - fashioned after European law, both Anglo-Saxon and Continental - permitted wife battering for the purpose of behaviour modification. The circumference of the stick used, specified the statute, should not exceed that of the husband's thumb.

Inevitably, many victims blame themselves for the dismal state of affairs. The abused party may have low self-esteem, a fluctuating sense of self-worth, primitive defence mechanisms, phobias, mental health problems, a disability, a history of failure, or a tendency to blame herself, or to feel inadequate (autoplastic neurosis).

She may have come from an abusive family or environment - which conditioned her to expect abuse as inevitable and "normal". In extreme and rare cases - the victim is a masochist, possessed of an urge to seek ill-treatment and pain. Gradually, the victims convert these unhealthy emotions and their learned helplessness in the face of persistent "gaslighting" into psychosomatic symptoms, anxiety and panic attacks, depression, or, in extremis, suicidal ideation and gestures.

From the Narcissistic Personality Disorders list - excerpt from my book "Toxic Relationships - Abuse and its Aftermath" (November 2005):

"Therapists, marriage counsellors, mediators, court-appointed guardians, police officers, and judges are human. Some of them are social reactionaries, others are narcissists, and a few are themselves spouse abusers. Many things work against the victim facing the justice system and the psychological profession.

Start with denial. Abuse is such a horrid phenomenon that society and its delegates often choose to ignore it or to convert it into a more benign manifestation, typically by pathologizing the situation or the victim - rather than the perpetrator.

A man's home is still his castle and the authorities are loath to intrude.

Most abusers are men and most victims are women. Even the most advanced communities in the world are largely patriarchal.

Misogynistic gender stereotypes, superstitions, and prejudices are strong.

Therapists are not immune to these ubiquitous and age-old influences and biases.

They are amenable to the considerable charm, persuasiveness, and manipulativeness of the abuser and to his impressive thespian skills. The abuser offers a plausible rendition of the events and interprets them to his favour. The therapist rarely has a chance to witness an abusive exchange first hand and at close quarters. In contrast, the abused are often on the verge of a nervous breakdown: harassed, unkempt, irritable, impatient, abrasive, and hysterical.

Confronted with this contrast between a polished, self-controlled, and suave abuser and his harried casualties – it is easy to reach the conclusion that the real victim is the abuser, or that both parties abuse each other equally. The prey's acts of self-defence, assertiveness, or insistence on her rights are interpreted as aggression, lability, or a mental health problem.

The profession's propensity to pathologize extends to the wrongdoers as well. Alas, few therapists are equipped to do proper clinical work, including diagnosis.

Abusers are thought by practitioners of psychology to be emotionally disturbed, the twisted outcomes of a history of familial violence and childhood traumas. They are typically diagnosed as suffering from a personality disorder, an inordinately low self-esteem, or codependence coupled with an all-devouring fear of abandonment. Consummate abusers use the right vocabulary and feign the appropriate 'emotions' and affect and, thus, sway the evaluator's judgement.

But while the victim's 'pathology' works against her – especially in custody battles – the culprit's 'illness' works for him, as a mitigating circumstance, especially in criminal proceedings."

In his seminal essay, "Understanding the Batterer in Visitation and Custody Disputes", Lundy Bancroft sums up the asymmetry in favour of the offender:

"Batterers ... adopt the role of a hurt, sensitive man who doesn't understand how things got so bad and just wants to work it all out 'for the good of the children'. He may cry ... and use language that demonstrates considerable insight into his own feelings. He is likely to be skilled at explaining how other people have turned the victim against him, and how she is denying him access to the children as a form of revenge... He commonly accuses her of having mental health problems, and may state that her family and friends agree with him ... that she is hysterical and that she is promiscuous. The abuser

tends to be comfortable lying, having years of practice, and so can sound believable when making baseless statements. The abuser benefits ... when professionals believe that they can 'just tell' who is lying and who is telling the truth, and so fail to adequately investigate.

Because of the effects of trauma, the victim of battering will often seem hostile, disjointed, and agitated, while the abuser appears friendly, articulate, and calm. Evaluators are thus tempted to conclude that the victim is the source of the problems in the relationship."

There is little the victim can do to "educate" the therapist or "prove" to him who is the guilty party. Mental health professionals are as ego-cantered as the next person. They are emotionally invested in opinions they form or in their interpretation of the abusive relationship. They perceive every disagreement as a challenge to their authority and are likely to pathologize such behaviour, labelling it "resistance" (or worse).

Why Good People Ignore Abuse

[Click here to view the video]

Why do good people - church-goers, pillars of the community, the salt of the earth - ignore abuse and neglect, even when it is on their doorstep and in their proverbial backyard (for instance, in hospitals, orphanages, shelters, prisons, and the like)?

Lack of Clear Definition

Perhaps because the word "abuse" is so ill-defined and so open to culture-bound interpretation.

We should distinguish functional abuse from the sadistic variety. The former is calculated to ensure outcomes or to punish transgressors. It is measured, impersonal, efficient, and disinterested.

The latter - the sadistic variety - fulfils the emotional needs of the perpetrator.

This distinction is often blurred. People feel uncertain and, therefore, reluctant to intervene. "The authorities know best" - they lie to themselves.

Avoiding the Unpleasant

People, good people, tend to avert their eyes from certain institutions which deal with anomalies and pain, death and illness - the unsavoury aspects of life which no one likes to be reminded of.

Like poor relatives, these institutions and events inside them are ignored and shunned.

The Common Guilt

Moreover, even good people abuse others habitually. Abusive conduct is so widespread that no one is exempt. Ours is a narcissistic - and, therefore, abusive - civilization.

People who find themselves caught up in anomic states - for instance, soldiers in war, nurses in hospitals, managers in corporations, parents or spouses in disintegrating families, or incarcerated inmates - tend to feel helpless and alienated. They experience a partial or total loss of control.

They are rendered vulnerable, powerless, and defenceless by events and circumstances beyond their influence.

Abuse amounts to exerting an absolute and all-pervasive domination of the victim's existence. It is a coping strategy employed by the abuser who wishes to reassert control over his life and, thus, to re-establish his mastery and superiority. By subjugating the victim - he regains his self-confidence and regulate his sense of self-worth.

Abuse as Catharsis

Even perfectly "normal" and good people (witness the events in the Abu Ghraib prison in Iraq) channel their negative emotions - pent up aggression, humiliation, rage, envy, diffuse hatred - and displace them.

The victims of abuse become symbols of everything that's wrong in the abuser's life and the situation he finds himself caught in. The act of abuse amounts to misplaced and violent venting.

The Wish to Conform and Belong - The Ethics of Peer Pressure

Many "good people" perpetrate heinous acts - or refrain from criticizing or opposing evil - out of a wish to conform. Abusing others is their way of demonstrating obsequious obeisance to authority, group affiliation, colleagueship, and adherence to the same ethical code of conduct and common values. They bask in the praise that is heaped on them by their superiors, fellow workers, associates, team mates, or collaborators.

Their need to belong is so strong that it overpowers ethical, moral, or legal considerations. They remain silent in the face of neglect, abuse, and atrocities because they feel insecure and they derive their identity almost entirely from the group.

Abuse rarely occurs where it does not have the sanction and blessing of the authorities, whether local or national. A permissive environment is sine qua non. The more abnormal the circumstances, the less normative the milieu, the further the scene of the crime is from public scrutiny - the more is egregious abuse likely to occur. This acquiescence is especially true in totalitarian societies where the use of physical force to discipline or eliminate dissent is an acceptable practice. But, unfortunately, it is also rampant in democratic societies.

Return

CHAPTER TWENTY ONE

Conning the System

Even a complete battery of tests, administered by experienced professionals sometimes fails to identify abusers and their personality disorders. Offenders are uncanny in their ability to deceive their evaluators. They often succeed in transforming therapists and diagnosticians into four types of collaborators: the adulators, the blissfully ignorant, the self-deceiving, and those deceived by the batterer's conduct or statements.

Abusers co-opt mental health and social welfare workers and compromise them – even when the diagnosis is unequivocal – by flattering them, by emphasizing common traits or a common background, by forming a joint front against the victim of abuse ("shared psychosis"), or by emotionally bribing them. Abusers are master manipulators and exploit the vulnerabilities, traumas, prejudices, and fears of the practitioners to "convert" them to the offender's cause.

The Adulators

The adulators are fully aware of the nefarious and damaging aspects of the abuser's behaviour but believe that they are more than offset by his positive traits and by the benefits to themselves, to their collective, or to society at large. They engage in an explicit trade-off between some of their principles and values and their personal profit, or the greater good. In a curious inversion of judgement, they cast the perpetrator as the victim of a smear campaign orchestrated by the abused, or attribute the offender's predicament to bigotry.

They mobilize to help the abuser; shield him from harm; do his chores for him; promote his agenda; connect him with like-minded people; and, in general, create the conditions and the environment for his success. This kind of alliance is especially prevalent in political parties, the government, multinationals, religious organizations and other hierarchical collectives.

The Ignorant

The blissfully ignorant are simply unaware of the "bad sides" of the abuser and they make sure to remain oblivious to them. They either look the other way, or pretend that the abuser's behaviour is normative, or turn a blind eye to his egregious misbehaviour.

They are classic deniers of reality. Some of them maintain a generally rosy outlook premised on the inbred benevolence of Mankind. Others simply cannot tolerate dissonance and discord. They prefer to live in a fantastic world where everything is harmonious and smooth and evil is banished. They react with rage to any information to the contrary and block it out instantly.

Once they had formed an opinion that the accusations against the abuser are overblown, malicious, and false – it becomes immutable. "I have made up my mind" – they seem to be broadcasting – "now do not confuse me with the facts". This type of denial is well evidenced in dysfunctional families.

The Self-deceivers

The self-deceivers are fully aware of the abuser's transgressions and malice, his indifference, lack of empathy, exploitativeness, and rampant grandiosity, but they prefer to displace the causes, or the effects of such misconduct. They attribute it to externalities ("a rough patch"), or judge it to be temporary. They even go as far as accusing the victim for the offender's lapses, or for defending herself ("she provoked him").

In a feat of cognitive dissonance, they deny any connection between the acts of the abuser and their consequences ("His wife abandoned him because she was promiscuous, not because of anything he did to her"). They are swayed by the barterer's undeniable charm, intelligence, or attractiveness. But the abuser needs not invest resources in converting them to his cause: he does not deceive them. They are self-propelled.

The Deceived

The deceived are people – or institutions, or collectives – deliberately taken for a premeditated ride by the abuser. He feeds them false information; manipulates their judgement; proffers plausible scenarios to account for his indiscretions; charms them; soils the opposition; appeals to their reason, or to their emotions; and promises the Moon.

Again, the abuser's incontrovertible powers of persuasion and his impressive personality play a part in this predatory ritual. The deceived are especially hard to deprogram. They are often themselves encumbered with abuser's traits and defences and find it impossible to admit to a mistake, or to atone. They are likely to persevere with the abuser to his and their bitter end.

[Read: The Guilt of the Abused: Pathologizing the Victim]

Note: The Risks of Self-diagnosis and Labelling

[Click here to watch the video]

The Narcissistic Personality Disorder (NPD) is a *disease*. It is defined *only* by and in the Diagnostic and Statistical Manual (DSM). All other "definitions" and compilations of "criteria" are irrelevant and very misleading.

People go around putting together lists of traits and behaviours (usually based on their experience with one person who was never officially diagnosed as a narcissist) and deciding that these lists constitute the essence or definition of narcissism.

People are erroneously using the term "narcissist" to describe every type of abuser or obnoxious and uncouth person. That is wrong. Not all abusers are narcissists.

Only a qualified mental health diagnostician can determine whether someone suffers from Narcissistic Personality Disorder (NPD) and this, following lengthy tests and personal interviews.

It is true that narcissists can mislead even the most experienced professional (see the article above). But this does not mean that laymen possess the ability to diagnose mental health disorders. The same signs and symptoms apply to many psychological problems and differentiating between them takes years of learning and training.

Return

CHAPTER TWENTY TWO

Befriending the System

In the process of mediation, marital therapy, or evaluation, counsellors frequently propose various techniques to ameliorate the abuse or bring it under control. Woe betides the party that dares object or turn these "recommendations" down. Thus, an abuse victim who declines to have any further contact with her batterer - is bound to be chastised by her therapist for obstinately refusing to constructively communicate with her violent spouse.

Better to play ball and adopt the sleek mannerisms of your abuser. Sadly, sometimes the only way to convince your therapist that it is not all in your head and that you are a victim - is by being insincere and by staging a well-calibrated performance, replete with the correct vocabulary. Therapists have Pavlovian reactions to certain phrases and theories and to certain "presenting signs and symptoms" (behaviours during the first few sessions). Learn these - and use them to your advantage. It is your only chance.

[Read the section: If You Have Common Children]

Phrases to Use

- "For the children's sake...";
- "I want to maintain constructive communications with my husband/wife";
- "The children need the ongoing presence of (the other parent)";
- "I wish to communicate/work with (the abuser) on our issues";
- "I wish to understand our relationship, help both sides achieve closure and get on with their lives/my life";
- "Healing process".

Things to Do

- Attend every session diligently. Never be late. Try not to cancel or reschedule meetings;

- Pay attention to your attire and makeup. Project a solid, conservative image. Do not make a dishevelled and disjointed appearance;
- Never argue with the counsellor or the evaluator or criticize them openly. If you have to disagree with him or her - do so elliptically and dispassionately;
- Agree to participate in a long-term treatment plan;
- Communicate with your abuser politely and reasonably. Do not let yourself get provoked! Do not throw temper tantrums or threaten anyone, not even indirectly! Restrain your hostility. Talk calmly and articulately. Count to ten or take a break, if you must;
- Repeatedly emphasize that the welfare and well-being of your children is uppermost in your mind - over and above any other (selfish) desire or consideration.

Maintain Your Boundaries

[See: Refuse All Contact]

Return

CHAPTER TWENTY THREE

Working with Professionals

Selecting the right professional is crucial. In the hands of an incompetent service provider, you may end up feeling abused all over again.

Go through the following check list before you settle on a divorce attorney, a financial consultant, a tax planner, a security adviser, or an accountant. Don't be ashamed to demand full disclosure - you have a right to do so. If you are met with impatience, arrogance, or a patronizing attitude - leave. This is not the right choice.

Make additional enquiries. Join online support groups and ask the members for recommendations. Visit directories on the Web - they are usually arranged by city, state, region, and country. Compare notes with others who have had similar experiences. Ask friends, neighbours, and family members to do the same. Scan the media for mentions of experts and mavens. Seek advice and referrals - the more the better.

Suggested Check List

Is the professional certified in your state/country? Can he himself fully represent you?

Will you be served by the expert himself - or by his staff? Don't end up being represented by someone you never even met! Make the professional's personal services an explicit condition in any written and verbal arrangement you make.

Obtain a complete financial offer, all fees and charges included, before you hire the services. Make sure you are aware of the full monetary implications of your decisions. Finding yourself financially stranded midway through is bad policy. If you can afford it - don't compromise and go for the best. But if you don't have the pecuniary means - don't overshoot.

What is the professional's track record? Does he have a long, varied, and successful experience in cases similar to yours? Don't hesitate to ask him or her for recommendations and referrals, testimonials and media clips.

What are the likely outcomes of the decisions you make, based on the specialist's recommendations? A true pro will never provide you with an iron-clad guarantee but neither will he dodge the question. Your expert should be able to give you a reasonably safe assessment of risks, rewards, potential and probable outcomes, and future developments.

Always enquire about different courses of action and substitute measures. Ask your professional why he prefers one method or approach to another and what is wrong with the alternatives. Don't accept his authority as the sole arbiter. Don't hesitate to argue with him and seek a second opinion if you are still not convinced.

Make the terms of your agreement crystal-clear, get it in writing, and in advance. Don't leave anything to chance or verbal understanding. Cover all grounds: the scope of activities, the fees, the termination clauses. Hiring a consultant is like getting married - you should also contemplate a possible divorce.

Relegate any inevitable contact with your abusive ex – when and where possible – to professionals: your lawyer, or your accountant. Work with professionals to extricate yourself and your loved ones from the quagmire of an abusive relationship.

Return

CHAPTER TWENTY FOUR

Interacting with Your Abuser

Having chosen your team of consultants and experts – and having hired their services – relegate any inevitable contact with your abusive ex – when and where possible – to professionals: your lawyer, or your accountant. Work with these qualified third parties to extricate yourself and your loved ones from the quagmire of an abusive relationship.

Be sure to maintain as much contact with your abuser as the courts, counsellors, mediators, guardians, or law enforcement officials' mandate. Do *not* contravene the decisions of the system. Work from the inside to change judgements, evaluations, or rulings – but *never* rebel against them or ignore them. You will only turn the system against you and your interests. But with the exception of the minimum mandated by the courts – decline any and all *gratuitous* contact with the narcissist.

Remember that many interactions are initiated by your abusive ex in order to trap or intimidate you. Keep referring him to your lawyer regarding legal issues, to your accountant or financial advisor concerning money matters, and to therapists, psychologists, and counsellors with regards to everything else (yourself and your common children).

Abusers react badly to such treatment. Yours will try to manipulate you into unintended contact. Do not respond to his pleading, romantic, nostalgic, flattering, or threatening e-mail and snail mail messages. Keep records of such correspondence and make it immediately available to the courts, law enforcement agencies, court-mandated evaluators, guardians ad litem, therapists, marital counsellors, child psychologist – and to your good friends. Keep him away by obtaining restraining orders and injunctions aplenty.

Abusers crave secrecy. Expose their misdeeds. Deter abuse by being open about your predicament. Share with like-minded others. It will ease your burden and keep him at bay, at least for awhile.

Your abusive ex-partner will try to dazzle you with attention. Return all gifts he sends you – unopened and unacknowledged. Keep your communications with him to the bare, cold, minimum. Do not be impolite or abusive – it is precisely how he wants you to behave. It may be used against you in a court of law. Keep your cool but be firm.

Do not let him re-enter your life surreptitiously. Stealth and ambient abuse are powerful tools. Refuse him entry to your premises. Do not even respond to the intercom. Do not talk to him on the phone. Hang up the minute you hear his voice while making clear to him, in a single, polite but unambiguous, sentence, that you are determined not to talk to him, that it's over for good.

Do not succumb to your weakness. It is tough living alone. You are bound to miss him horribly at times, selectively recalling only the good moments and the affection in your doomed relationship. Do not "dip" into the poisonous offerings of your abuser. Do not relapse. Be strong. Fill your life with new hobbies, new interests, new friends, new loves, and a new purpose.

Do not visit your abuser on "special occasions", or in emergencies. Do not let him convince you to celebrate an anniversary, a birthday, a successful business transaction, a personal achievement or triumph. Do not let him turn your own memories against you. Do not visit him in the hospital, in jail, a rehab centre, or join him in a memorial service.

Do not ask him for anything, even if you are in dire need. When you are forced to meet him, do not discuss your personal affairs – or his. Your abuser's friendship is fake, his life with you a confabulation, his intentions dishonest and dishonourable. He is the enemy.

Abuse by proxy continues long after the relationship is officially over (at least as far as you are concerned). Do not respond to questions, requests, or pleas forwarded to you through third parties. Disconnect from third parties whom you know are spying on you at his behest. Do not discuss him with your children. Do not gossip about him.

The majority of abusers get the message, however belatedly and reluctantly. Others – more vindictive and obsessed – continue to haunt their quarry for years to come. These are the stalkers.

[Read: Coping with Your Abuser and Coping with Your Stalker]

Return

CHAPTER TWENTY FIVE

Abusing the Gullible Narcissist

"Such a one (the narcissist – SV) is encased, is he not, in an armour – such an armour! The armour of the crusaders was nothing to it – an armour of arrogance, of pride, of complete self-esteem. This armour, it is in some ways a protection, the arrows, the everyday arrows of life glance off it. But there is this danger; Sometimes a man in armour might not even know he was being attacked. He will be slow to see, slow to hear – slower still to feel."
["Dead Man's Mirror" by Agatha Christie in "Hercule Poirot – The Complete Short Stories", Great Britain, HarperCollins Publishers, 1999]

The irony is that narcissists, who consider themselves worldly, discerning, knowledgeable, shrewd, erudite, and astute, are actually more gullible than the average person. This is because the narcissist is a fake: his Self is <u>False</u>, his life a <u>confabulation</u>, his reality test gone. Narcissists live in a fantasyland all their own in which they are the centre of the universe, admired, feared, held in awe, and respected for their omnipotence and omniscience.

Narcissists are prone to magical thinking. They hold themselves immune to the consequences of their actions (or inaction) and, therefore, beyond punishment and the laws of Man. Narcissists are easily persuaded to assume unreasonable risks and expect miracles to happen. They often find themselves on the receiving end of investment scams, for instance.

Narcissists feel entitled to money, power, and honours incommensurate with their accomplishments or toil. The world, or God, or the nation, or society, or their families, co-workers, employers, even neighbours owe them a trouble-free, exalted, and luxurious existence. They are rudely shocked when they are penalized for their misconduct or when their fantasies remain just that.

The narcissist believes that he is destined to greatness – or at least the easy life. He wakes up every morning fully ready for a fortuitous stroke of luck. That explains the narcissist's reckless behaviours and his lazed lack of self-discipline. It also explains why he is so easily duped and why he ends his life a bitter, disillusioned man.

By playing on the narcissist's grandiosity and paranoia, it is possible to deceive and manipulate him effortlessly. Just offer him Narcissistic Supply – admiration, affirmation, adulation – and he is yours. Harp on his insecurities and his persecutory delusions, and he is likely to trust only you and cling to you for dear life.

Narcissists attract abuse. Haughty, exploitative, demanding, insensitive, and quarrelsome, they tend to draw opprobrium and provoke anger and even hatred. Sorely lacking in interpersonal skills, devoid of empathy, and steeped in irksome grandiose fantasies, they invariably fail to mitigate the irritation and revolt that they induce in others.

Successful narcissists are frequently targeted by stalkers and erotomaniacs: usually mentally-ill people who develop a fixation on the narcissist of a sexual or emotional nature. When these avid and delusional pursuers are inevitably rebuffed by the narcissist, they become vindictive and even violent.

Less prominent narcissists end up sharing life with codependents and Inverted Narcissists.

The narcissist's situation is exacerbated by the fact that, often, the narcissist himself is an abuser. Like the boy who cried "wolf", people do not believe that the perpetrator of egregious deeds can himself fall prey to maltreatment. They tend to ignore and discard the narcissist's cries for help and disbelieve his protestations.

Narcissists react to abuse as other victims do. Traumatized, the narcissist goes through the phases of denial, helplessness, rage, depression, and acceptance. But, his reactions are amplified by his shattered sense of omnipotence. Abuse breeds humiliation. To the narcissist, helplessness is a novel experience.

The narcissistic defence mechanisms and their behavioural manifestations and correlates – diffuse rage, idealization and devaluation, exploitation – are useless when confronted with a determined, vindictive, or delusional stalker or a well-honed con artist. That the narcissist is flattered by the attention he receives from the abuser, renders him more vulnerable to the latter's manipulation.

Nor can the narcissist come to terms with his need for help or acknowledge that wrongful behaviour on his part may have contributed somehow to the situation. His self-image as a mighty, infallible, all-knowing person, far superior to others, won't let him own up to shortfalls or mistakes.

As the abuse progresses, the narcissist feels increasingly cornered. His conflicting emotional needs – to preserve the integrity of his grandiose False Self even as he seeks much needed succour and support – place an unbearable strain on the precarious balance of his immature personality. Decompenzation (the disintegration of the narcissist's defence mechanisms) leads to acting out and, if the abuse is protracted, to withdrawal and even to psychotic micro-episodes.

Abusive acts in themselves are rarely dangerous. Not so the reactions to abuse – above all, the overwhelming sense of violation and humiliation.

[Read more in the section Manipulate Him]

Return

CHAPTER TWENTY SIX

The Three Forms of Closure

For her traumatic wounds to heal, the victim of abuse requires closure: one final interaction with her tormentor in which he, hopefully, acknowledges his misbehaviour and even tenders an apology. Fat chance. Few abusers – especially if they are <u>narcissistic</u> – are amenable to such weakling pleasantries. More often, the abused are left to wallow in a poisonous stew of misery, self-pity, and <u>self-recrimination</u>.

Depending on the severity, duration, and nature of the abuse, there are three forms of effective closure:

Conceptual Closure

This most common variant involves a frank dissection of the abusive relationship. The parties meet to analyse what went wrong, to allocate blame and guilt, to derive lessons, and to part ways cathartically cleansed. In such an exchange, a compassionate offender (quite the oxymoron, admittedly) offers his prey the chance to rid herself of cumulating resentment.

He also disabuses her of the notion that she, in any way, had been guilty or responsible for her maltreatment; that it was all her fault; that she deserved to be punished; and that she could have saved the relationship (<u>malignant optimism</u>). With this burden gone, the victim is ready to resume her life and to seek love and companionship elsewhere.

Retributive Closure

When the abuse has been "gratuitous" (<u>sadistic</u>), repeated, and protracted, conceptual closure is far from enough. Retribution is called for, an element of vengeance, of restorative justice and a restored balance. Recuperation hinges on punishing the delinquent and merciless party. The penal intervention of the Law is often therapeutic to the abused.

Some victims smugly delude themselves into believing that their abuser assuredly is experiencing guilt and conscience pangs (which is rarely the case). They revel in his ostensible self-inflicted torment. His sleepless nights become their sweet revenge.

Regrettably, the victim's understandable emotions often lead to abusive (and illegal) acts. Many of the tormented stalk their erstwhile abusers and take the law into their own hands. Abuse tends to breed abuse all around, in both prey and predator.

Dissociative Closure

Absent the other two forms of closure, victims of egregious and prolonged mistreatment tend to repress their painful memories. In extremis, they dissociate. Dissociative Identity Disorder (DID) – formerly known as "Multiple Personality Disorder" – is thought to be such a reaction. The harrowing experiences are "sliced off", tucked away, and attributed to "another personality".

Sometimes, the victim "assimilates" his tormentor, and even openly and consciously identifies with him. This is a narcissistic defence. In his own anguished mind, the victim becomes omnipotent and, therefore, invulnerable. He develops a False Self. The True Self is, thus, shielded from further harm and injury.

According to several psychodynamic theories of psychopathology, repressed content rendered unconscious is the cause of all manner of mental health disorders. The victim thus pays a hefty price for avoiding and evading his or her predicament.

Return

CHAPTER TWENTY SEVEN

Back to La-la Land

Giving the Narcissist a Second Chance

Relationships with narcissists peter out slowly and tortuously. Narcissists do not provide closure. They stalk. They cajole, beg, promise, persuade, and, ultimately, succeed in doing the impossible yet again: sweep you off your feet, though you know better than to succumb to their spurious and superficial charms.

So, you go back to your "relationship" and hope for a better ending. You walk on eggshells. You become the epitome of submissiveness, a perfect Source of Narcissistic Supply, the ideal mate, or spouse, or partner, or colleague. You gingerly keep your fingers crossed.

But how does the narcissist react to the resurrection of the bond?

It depends on whether you have re-entered the liaison from a position or strength, or of vulnerability and weakness.

The narcissist casts all interactions with other people in terms of conflicts or competitions to be won. He does not regard you as a partner, but as an adversary to be subjugated and defeated. Thus, as far as he is concerned, your return to the fold is a clear triumph, proof of his superiority and irresistibility.

If he perceives you as autonomous, dangerously independent, and capable of bailing out and abandoning him, the narcissist acts the part of the sensitive, empathic, compassionate, and loving counterpart. Narcissists respect strength, they are awed by it. As long as you maintain a "no nonsense" attitude, placing the narcissist on probation, he is likely to behave himself.

If, on the other hand, you have resumed contact because you have capitulated to his threats or because you are manifestly dependent on him financially or emotionally, the narcissist will pounce on your frailty and exploit your fragility to the maximum. Following a perfunctory honeymoon, he will immediately seek to control and abuse you.

In both cases, the narcissist's thespian reserves are ultimately exhausted and his true nature and feelings emerge. The facade crumbles and beneath it lurks the same old heartless falsity that is the narcissist. His gleeful smugness at having bent you to his wishes and rules; his all-consuming sense of entitlement; his sexual depravity; his aggression, pathological envy, and rage – all erupt uncontrollably.

The prognosis for the renewed affair is far worse if it follows a lengthy separation in which you have made a life for yourself with your own interests, pursuits, set of friends, needs, wishes, plans, and obligations, independent of your narcissistic ex.

The narcissist cannot countenance your separateness. To him, you are a mere instrument of gratification or an extension of his bloated False Self. He resents your pecuniary wherewithal; is insanely jealous of your friends; refuses to accept your preferences or compromise his own; is envious and dismissive of your accomplishments.

Ultimately, the fact that you have survived without his constant presence seems to deny him his much-needed Narcissistic Supply. He rides the inevitable cycle of idealization and devaluation. He berates you; humiliates you in public; threatens you; destabilizes you by behaving unpredictably; fosters ambient abuse; and uses others to intimidate and humble you ("abuse by proxy").

You are then faced with a tough choice:

To leave again and be forced to give up all the emotional and financial investments that went into your attempt to resurrect the relationship - or to go on trying, subject to daily abuse, conflict, and worse?

It is a well-known landscape. You have been here before. But this familiarity doesn't make it less nightmarish.

Return

THE AUTHOR

Shmuel (Sam) Vaknin

Curriculum Vitae

Born in 1961 in Qiryat-Yam, Israel

Served in the Israeli Defence Force (1979-1982) in training and education units

Full proficiency in Hebrew and in English

Education

1970 to 1978

Completed nine semesters in the Technion – Israel Institute of Technology, Haifa

1982 to 1983

Ph.D. in Philosophy (dissertation: "Time Asymmetry Revisited") – California Miramar University, California, USA
(formerly: Pacific Western University)

1982 to 1985

Graduate of numerous courses in Finance Theory and International Trading in the UK and USA.

Certified in Psychological Counselling Techniques by Brainbench

Certified E-Commerce Concepts Analyst by Brainbench

Certified Financial Analyst by Brainbench

Business Experience

1980 to 1983

Founder and co-owner of a chain of computerized information kiosks in Tel-Aviv, Israel

1982 to 1985

Senior positions with the Nessim D. Gaon Group of Companies in Geneva, Paris and New-York (NOGA and APROFIM SA):
- Chief Analyst of Edible Commodities in the Group's Headquarters in Switzerland
- Manager of the Research and Analysis Division
- Manager of the Data Processing Division
- Project Manager of the Nigerian Computerized Census
- Vice President in charge of RND and Advanced Technologies
- Vice President in charge of Sovereign Debt Financing

1985 to 1986

Represented Canadian Venture Capital Funds in Israel

1986 to 1987

General Manager of IPE Ltd. in London. The firm financed international multi-lateral countertrade and leasing transactions.

1988 to 1990

Co-founder and Director of "Mikbats-Tesuah", a portfolio management firm based in Tel-Aviv

Activities included large-scale portfolio management, underwriting, forex trading and general financial advisory services.

1990 to Present

Freelance consultant to many of Israel's Blue-Chip firms, mainly on issues related to the capital markets in Israel, Canada, the UK and the USA.

Consultant to foreign RND ventures and to Governments on macro-economic matters

Freelance journalist in various media in the United States

1990 to 1995

President of the Israel chapter of the Professors World Peace Academy (PWPA) and (briefly) Israel representative of the "Washington Times"

1993 to 1994

Co-owner and Director of many business enterprises:
- The Omega and Energy Air-conditioning Concern
- AVP Financial Consultants
- Handiman Legal Services - Total annual turnover of the group: 10 million USD.

Co-owner, Director and Finance Manager of COSTI Ltd. - Israel's largest computerized information vendor and developer. Raised funds through a series of private placements locally in the USA, Canada and London.

1993 to 1996

Publisher and Editor of a Capital Markets Newsletter distributed by subscription only to dozens of subscribers countrywide

Tried and incarcerated for 11 months for his role in an attempted takeover of Israel's Agriculture Bank involving securities fraud.

Managed the Internet and International News Department of an Israeli mass media group, "Ha-Tikshoret and Namer"

Assistant in the Law Faculty in Tel-Aviv University (to Prof. S.G. Shoham)

1996 to 1999

Financial consultant to leading businesses in Macedonia, Russia and the Czech Republic

Economic commentator in "Nova Makedonija", "Dnevnik", "Makedonija Denes", "Izvestia", "Argumenti i Fakti", "The Middle East Times", "The New Presence", "Central Europe Review", and other periodicals, and in the economic programs on various channels of Macedonian Television.

Chief Lecturer in courses in Macedonia organized by the Agency of Privatization, by the Stock Exchange, and by the Ministry of Trade

1999 to 2002

Economic Advisor to the Government of the Republic of Macedonia and to the Ministry of Finance

2001 to 2003

Senior Business Correspondent for United Press International (UPI)

2005 to Present

Associate Editor and columnist, Global Politician

Founding Analyst, The Analyst Network

Contributing Writer, The American Chronicle Media Group

Expert, Self-growth and Bizymoms and contributor to Mental Health Matters

2007 to 2008

Columnist and analyst in "Nova Makedonija", "Fokus", and "Kapital" (Macedonian papers and newsweeklies)

2008 to 2011

Member of the Steering Committee for the Advancement of Healthcare in the Republic of Macedonia

Advisor to the Minister of Health of Macedonia

Seminars and lectures on economic issues in various forums in Macedonia

Contributor to CommentVision

2011 to Present

Editor in Chief of Global Politician

Columnist in Dnevnik and Publika (Macedonia)

Columnist in InfoPlus

Member CFACT Board of Advisors

Contributor to Recovering the Self

Web and Journalistic Activities

Author of extensive Web sites in:
- Psychology ("Malignant Self-love: Narcissism Revisited") - an Open Directory Cool Site for 8 years
- Philosophy ("Philosophical Musings")
- Economics and Geopolitics ("World in Conflict and Transition")

Owner of the Narcissistic Abuse Study List, the Toxic Relationships List, and the Abusive Relationships Newsletter (more than 7,000 members)

Owner of the Economies in Conflict and Transition Study List and the Links and Factoid Study List

Editor of mental health disorders and Central and Eastern Europe categories in various Web directories (Open Directory, Search Europe, Mentalhelp.net)

Editor of the Personality Disorders, Narcissistic Personality Disorder, the Verbal and Emotional Abuse, and the Spousal (Domestic) Abuse and Violence topics on Suite 101 and contributing author on Bellaonline.

Columnist and commentator in "The New Presence", United Press International (UPI), InternetContent, eBookWeb, PopMatters, Global Politician, The Analyst Network, Conservative Voice, The American Chronicle Media Group, eBookNet.org, and "Central Europe Review".

Publications and Awards

"Managing Investment Portfolios in States of Uncertainty", Limon Publishers, Tel-Aviv, 1988

"The Gambling Industry", Limon Publishers, Tel-Aviv, 1990

"Requesting My Loved One: Short Stories", Miskal-Yedioth Aharonot, Tel-Aviv, 1997

"The Suffering of Being Kafka" (electronic book of Hebrew and English Short Fiction), Prague, 1998-2004

"The Macedonian Economy at a Crossroads – On the Way to a Healthier Economy" (dialogues with Nikola Gruevski), Skopje, 1998

"The Exporter's Pocketbook" Ministry of Trade, Republic of Macedonia, Skopje, 1999

"Malignant Self-love: Narcissism Revisited", Narcissus Publications, Prague and Skopje, 1999-2013 (Read excerpts - click here)

The Narcissism, Psychopathy, and Abuse in Relationships Series (electronic books regarding relationships with abusive narcissists and psychopaths), Prague, 1999-2013

"After the Rain – How the West Lost the East", Narcissus Publications in association with Central Europe Review/CEENMI, Prague and Skopje, 2000

Personality Disorders Revisited (electronic book about personality disorders), Prague, 2007

More than 30 e-books about psychology, international affairs, business and economics, philosophy, short fiction, and reference (free downloads here)

Winner of numerous awards, among them Israel's Council of Culture and Art Prize for Maiden Prose (1997), The Rotary Club Award for Social Studies (1976), and the Bilateral Relations Studies Award of the American Embassy in Israel (1978).

Hundreds of articles in all fields of finance, political economics, and geopolitics, published in both print and Web periodicals in many countries.

Many appearances in the electronic and print media on subjects in psychology, philosophy, and the sciences, and concerning economic matters.

Write to Me:

samvaknin@gmail.com

narcissisticabuse-owner@yahoogroups.com

My Web Sites:

Economy/Politics:

http://ceeandbalkan.tripod.com/

Psychology:

http://www.narcissistic-abuse.com/

Philosophy:

http://philosophos.tripod.com/

Poetry:

http://samvak.tripod.com/contents.html

Fiction:

http://samvak.tripod.com/sipurim.html

Participate in discussions about Abusive Relationships:

https://plus.google.com/communities/116582645889927140499

http://www.runboard.com/bnarcissisticabuserecovery

http://thepsychopath.freeforums.org/

The Narcissistic Abuse Study List

http://health.groups.yahoo.com/group/narcissisticabuse/

The Toxic Relationships Study List

http://groups.yahoo.com/group/toxicrelationships

Abusive Relationships Newsletter

http://groups.google.com/group/narcissisticabuse/

**Follow my work on NARCISSISTS and PSYCHOPATHS
As well as international affairs and economics**

Be my friend on **Facebook**:

http://www.facebook.com/samvaknin

Subscribe to my **YouTube** channel (280 videos about narcissists and psychopaths and abuse in relationships):

http://www.youtube.com/samvaknin

Subscribe to my other **YouTube** channel (100 videos about international affairs, economics, and philosophy):

http://www.youtube.com/vakninmusings

Subscribe to my **YouTube** channel Vaknin Says:

http://www.youtube.com/vakninsays

You may also with to join Malignant Self-love: Narcissism Revisited on **Facebook** and **Google Plus**:

http://www.facebook.com/pages/Malignant-Self-Love-Narcissism-Revisited/50634038043 or

https://www.facebook.com/NarcissusPublications

http://www.facebook.com/narcissistpsychopathabuse

https://plus.google.com/u/0/111189140058482892878/posts

Follow me on **Twitter**, **MySpace**, **Google Plus**, **Pinterest**, **Tumblr**, **SoCl**, **Linkedin**, or **FriendFeed**:

http://www.twitter.com/samvaknin

http://www.myspace.com/samvaknin

https://plus.google.com/115041965408538110094

http://pinterest.com/samvaknin/the-psychopathic-narcissist-and-his-world/

http://narcissistpsychopath-abuse.tumblr.com/

http://www.so.cl/#/profile/Sam-Vaknin

http://www.linkedin.com/in/samvaknin

http://www.friendfeeed.com/samvaknin

Subscribe to my **Scribd** page: dozens of books for download at no charge to you!

http://www.scribd.com/samvaknin

Return

Abused? Stalked? Harassed? Bullied? Victimized?
Afraid? Confused? Need HELP? DO SOMETHING ABOUT IT!

Brought up by a Narcissistic Parent?
Married to a Narcissist – or Divorcing One?
Afraid your Children will turn out to be the same?
Want to cope with this pernicious, baffling condition?
OR
Are You a Narcissist – or suspect that you are one...
These books and video lectures will teach you how to...
Cope, Survive, and Protect Your Loved Ones!

We offer you three types of products:

I. **"Malignant Self-love: Narcissism Revisited"** (the print edition) via Barnes and Noble or directly from the publisher;

II. **E-books** (electronic files to be read on a computer, laptop, NOOK, or Kindle e-reader devices, or smartphone); and

III. **DVDs** with video lectures.

I. PRINT EDITION

1. From BARNES and NOBLE

You can buy the PRINT edition of "Malignant Self-love: Narcissism Revisited" (May 2013) from Barnes and Noble (the cheapest option, but does not include a bonus pack):

http://search.barnesandnoble.com/bookSearch/isbnInquiry.asp?r=1&ISBN=9788023833843

Or, click on this link - http://www.bn.com - and search for "Sam Vaknin" or "Malignant Self-love".

2. From the PUBLISHER

"Malignant Self-love: Narcissism Revisited" is now available also from the publisher (more expensive, but includes a bonus pack):

More information:

http://www.narcissistic-abuse.com/thebook.html

To purchase - click on this link:

http://www.ccnow.com/cgi-local/cart.cgi?vaksam_MSL

II. ELECTRONIC BOOKS (e-Books)

An electronic book is a computer file, sent to you as an attachment to an e-mail message. Just save it to your hard disk, smartphone, or e-reader (Kindle, NOOK) and click on the file to open, read, and learn!

A library of Kindle e-books about narcissists, psychopaths, and abuse in relationships and the workplace – click on this link to purchase the titles.

To purchase the e-books click on these links:

"The Narcissism Series"

Save 63$! Buy SIXTEEN electronic books (e-books) regarding Pathological Narcissism, relationships with abusive narcissists and psychopaths, and Narcissistic Personality Disorder (NPD):

http://www.ccnow.com/cgi-local/cart.cgi?vaksam_SERIES

You can also purchase some of the books comprising the Narcissism Series separately:

1. "The Narcissist and Psychopath in the Workplace"
   http://www.ccnow.com/cgi-local/cart.cgi?vaksam_WORKPLACE

2. "Abusive Relationships WORKBOOK"
   http://www.ccnow.com/cgi-local/cart.cgi?vaksam_WORKBOOK

3. "Toxic Relationships: Abuse and its Aftermath"
   http://www.ccnow.com/cgi-local/cart.cgi?vaksam_ABUSE

4. NEW!!! "The Narcissist and Psychopath in Therapy"
   http://www.ccnow.com/cgi-local/cart.cgi?vaksam_THERAPY

5. "Malignant Self-love: Narcissism Revisited"
   NINTH, Revised Edition - FULL TEXT
   http://www.ccnow.com/cgi-local/cart.cgi?vaksam_MSL-EBOOK

6. "Pathological Narcissism FAQs (Frequently Asked Questions)"
   http://www.ccnow.com/cgi-local/cart.cgi?vaksam_FAQS

7. "The World of the Narcissist"
   http://www.ccnow.com/cgi-local/cart.cgi?vaksam_ESSAY

8. "Excerpts from the Archives of the Narcissism List"
   http://www.ccnow.com/cgi-local/cart.cgi?vaksam_EXCERPTS

9. "Diary of a Narcissist"
   http://www.ccnow.com/cgi-local/cart.cgi?vaksam_JOURNAL

"Personality Disorders Revisited"

450 pages about Borderline, Narcissistic, Antisocial-Psychopathic, Histrionic, Paranoid, Obsessive-Compulsive, Schizoid, Schizotypal, Masochistic, Sadistic, Depressive, Negativistic-Passive-Aggressive, Dependent, and other Personality Disorders!

Click on this link to purchase the ebook:

http://www.ccnow.com/cgi-local/cart.cgi?vaksam_PERSONALITY

NEW!!! How to Divorce a Narcissist or a Psychopath

Divorcing a narcissist or a psychopath is no easy or dangerless task. This book is no substitute for legal aid, though it does provide copious advice on anything from hiring an attorney, to domestic violence shelters, planning your getaway, involving the police, and obtaining restraining orders. Issues from court-mandated evaluation to custody are elaborated upon. The book describes the psychology of psychopathic narcissists, paranoids, bullies and stalkers and guides you through dozens of coping strategies and techniques, especially if you have shared children.

Click on this link now:

http://www.ccnow.com/cgi-local/cart.cgi?vaksam_DIVORCEABUSER

New eBook! How to Cope with Narcissistic and Psychopathic Abusers and Stalkers

How to cope with stalkers, bullies, narcissists, psychopaths, and other abusers in the family, community, and workplace; how to navigate a system, which is often hostile to the victim: the courts, law enforcement (police), psychotherapists, evaluators, and social or welfare services; tips, advice, and information.

Click on this link now:

http://www.ccnow.com/cgi-local/cart.cgi?vaksam_COPING

III. Video Lectures on DVDs

Purchase **3 DVDs** with 16 hours of video lectures on narcissists, psychopaths, and abuse in relationships - click on this link:

http://www.ccnow.com/cgi-local/cart.cgi?vaksam_DVD

Save 73$! Purchase the **3 DVDs** (16 hours of video lectures) + The Narcissism, Psychopathy and Abuse in Relationships Series of **SIXTEEN e-BOOKS** - click on this link:

http://www.ccnow.com/cgi-local/cart.cgi?vaksam_DVDSERIES

Purchase the **3 DVDs** (16 hours of video lectures) + the print book **"Malignant Self-love: Narcissism Revisited"** (ninth print edition) - click on this link:

http://www.ccnow.com/cgi-local/cart.cgi?vaksam_DVDPRINT

Free excerpts from the NINTH, Revised Impression of "Malignant Self-love: Narcissism Revisited" are available as well as a **NEW EDITION of the Narcissism Book of Quotes.**

Click on this link to download the files:

http://www.narcissistic-abuse.com/freebooks.html

Download Free Electronic Books - click on this link:

http://www.narcissistic-abuse.com/freebooks.html

Additional Resources

Testimonials and Additional Resources

You can read Readers' Reviews at the Barnes and Noble Web page dedicated to "Malignant Self-love" – HERE:

http://search.barnesandnoble.com/bookSearch/isbnInquiry.asp?r=1&ISBN=9788023833843

Links to Therapist Directories, Psychological Tests, NPD Resources, Support Groups for Narcissists and Their Victims, and Tutorials

http://health.groups.yahoo.com/group/narcissisticabuse/message/5458

Support Groups for Victims of Narcissists and Narcissists

http://dmoz.org/Health/Mental_Health/Disorders/Personality/Narcissistic

Printed in Poland
by Amazon Fulfillment
Poland Sp. z o.o., Wrocław